BASIC ECONOMICS

BASIC ECONOMICS

IN A

DEMOCRATIC SOCIETY USING

A MACHINE TECHNOLOGY

BY

JAMES GILBERT EVANS, JR.

CHAPEL HILL
THE UNIVERSITY OF NORTH CAROLINA PRESS
1934

COPYRIGHT, 1934, BY
JAMES GILBERT EVANS, JR.

PRINTED AND BOUND IN THE UNITED STATES OF AMERICA
BY THE SEEMAN PRINTERY, INC., DURHAM, NORTH CAROLINA

PREFACE

This book is an approach to the study of economics from the point of view of the interests of a democratic society using a machine-power technology. The questions asked here are first, what are our resources, physical, technological, and cultural? second, how can these resources be used to best advantage, that is, to get economic goods produced and distributed as they are needed?

In the usual approach to the subject it is assumed that human nature is invariable; that the best economic system is one in which the individual has the greatest freedom; and that the exercise of individual freedom will in some way result in the greatest good to society. It was necessary for the economic system justified on this theory to come to the verge of complete collapse and remain there for years before teachers of the subject generally began to take full cognizance of the fact that economic freedom for the individual had long ago disappeared, if it had ever existed at all, and that the "human nature" of the laissez faire era was perhaps more natural than human, more like the jungle and its customs than like civilized man. As one of those who has taught the "principles of economics," I am not in a position to read a lesson to others who have done no better. But if the teacher cannot foresee disaster, he can at least become aware of it when it arrives. He can make the effort to see the world of economic phenomena through his own eyes. If he does so honestly and intelligently, I believe he will have to ask again and attempt to answer the questions considered in this book.

J. G. E.

Chapel Hill, North Carolina
October 22, 1934

CONTENTS

CHAPTER   PAGE

PART I

THE THEORY OF SOCIAL ECONOMICS IN RESOURCE UTILIZATION

INTRODUCTION 3
   I. SOCIAL EFFECTIVENESS IN RESOURCE UTILIZATION............. 9
  II. THE PROCESS OF RESOURCE UTILIZATION..................... 16
 III. THE LAW OF DIMINISHING RETURNS......................... 24
 IV. THE LAW OF COMPARATIVE ADVANTAGE....................... 37
  V. LEAST-MONEY-COST COMBINATION OF RESOURCES.............. 47

PART II

ESSENTIAL ECONOMIC FUNCTIONS IN RESOURCE UTILIZATION

INTRODUCTION 69
 VI. RELATIVE VOLUMES OF RESOURCES........................... 70
VII. A COMMON DENOMINATOR OF COMPARISON: MONEY............. 80
VIII. THE PRICING PROCESS..................................... 91
 IX. PRICING GOODS FOR CONSUMPTION.......................... 96
  X. THE PRICING OF RESOURCES................................ 104

PART III

INSTRUMENTAL ECONOMICS

 XI. ECONOMICS: SCIENCE, METHOD, AND ART..................... 113
XII. THE BACKGROUND OF ECONOMICS TODAY...................... 121

BASIC ECONOMICS

PART I. THEORY OF SOCIAL ECONOMICS

INTRODUCTION

RESOURCES AND THEIR UTILIZATION

NEEDS

FOR many thousands of years mankind has not considered the gratuitous offering of nature sufficient for a satisfactory human existence. Particular kinds of food, clothing, shelter, recreation, and other goods have been considered worth the human effort necessary to obtain them. Those goods, both tangible and intangible, which individuals and groups deem essential to the good life have become the means of meeting needs.[2] The character of needs at any particular time or place is determined by the requirements for human life itself, by the realities of the environment which limit the range and volume of goods it is reasonably possible to obtain, and by man's ability to imagine the requirements for a better existence. When there has seemed no way to provide more than a bare existence for the masses of people, the sting of privation and suffering has been mitigated by the idealization of poverty and by an emphasis upon spiritual rather than material well-being. Wars and other methods of human slaughter have been condoned if starvation threatened. In recent generations it has become possible to provide more than mere subsistence for all members of society. At the same time we have come to believe that material well-being is an essential for the good life and that all forms of human slaughter are unnecessary.

But new needs are so easily imagined and they become so pervasive, especially in a democratic society, that many have

[1] Theory is here used to mean an analysis of a given set of factors in their ideal relations with one another. Our task is to analyze the factors which influence the economizing of resources from the social point of view, that is, to analyze the ideal relations between needs and resources.

[2] The term "goods" as used here includes everything that contributes directly to human needs, both commodities and services. Some goods may not require human effort to obtain but most of them do. The air is "free" until we want it heated or cooled in greater degree than nature provides. A "good" is a single commodity or service.

remained unfilled in all generations. It has never been possible to provide all individuals and groups with everything considered desirable. Consequently it has always been necessary to get as much as possible of what was needed from the environment by *economizing*, that is, by maximizing the results of human effort.[3]

RESOURCES

To aid in the process of providing for a satisfactory existence mankind has, through the ages, accumulated knowledge, skills, material objects, and social organization. These accumulations comprise human culture; they enable us to utilize soils, minerals, waters, forests, more effectively. All the elements of the environment which help to provide goods for the meeting of needs are resources—human, natural, and cultural.

1. Human resources consist of the mental and physical effort, which brings about the existence of some and the utilization of all other resources.

2. Natural resources are all those contributing elements of the environment which are not dependent upon human effort for their existence.

3. Cultural resources consist of:[4]

a. Material objects which have come into existence as a result of human effort—machinery, tools, livestock, railroads, highways, buildings of all kinds, and many others which help in obtaining more goods for consumption—and also the food, clothing, homes, and other objects which are immediately available for use;

b. Knowledge of the phenomena of the natural and human resources which enables their more effective utilization;[5]

c. Social arrangements, institutions, practices, or customs which determine the rights and duties as well as the liberties and exposures of individuals and groups in the economic process.[6]

---

[3] To economize is to use to the best advantage.

[4] "The various elements of culture may be classified as material tools; social structure; sentiments, values, attitudes, and *mores;* activities or skills; symbols; and beliefs or intellectual elements." J. K. Folsom, *Culture and Social Progress,* p. 34. (Longmans, Green & Company, 1928).

[5] Phenomena are facts, occurrences or circumstances observed or observable. A fact is a truth known by actual observation or authorative testimony.

[6] The exposures of an individual or group to the liberties of others.

BASIC ECONOMIC PROBLEMS

The use of resources to obtain goods is *production;* the division of goods among the members of society is *sharing* or *distribution;* the actual use of goods to fill needs is *consumption.* In carrying on these phases of resources utilization every human society is faced with the following basic problems which must be solved in some manner through individual and collective organization and action:

1. How shall resources be combined and controlled so as to produce as many needed goods as possible and at the same time give proper recognition to the influence of work and working conditions on those who labor, and to the resource needs of future generations?

2. What kinds of goods shall be produced and in what quantities?

3. How shall the goods that are produced be divided for consumption among the members of society?

DYNAMIC FACTORS IN ECONOMIC ORGANIZATION

In solving these problems, every human society creates a set of arrangements, institutions, and practices which comprise what is known as an *economic order* or *system.*[7] The sort of order or system which a society will create for the purpose of organizing economic activity depends upon the nature and interaction of certain dynamic or causal factors. These may be grouped into three general types:

First, there are the *social objectives,* aims, or purposes in the production, sharing and consumption of goods which are reflected in the dominating concepts of a satisfactory existence, the good life, or individual and group well-being, and which

[7] "Institution is a verbal symbol which for want of a better describes a cluster of social usages. It connotes a way of thought or action of some prevalence and permanence, which is imbedded in the habits of a group or the customs of a people. In ordinary speech it is another word for procedure, convention or arrangement; in the language of books it is the singular of what the mores and folkways are the plural. Institutions fix the confines of and impose form upon the activities of human beings. The world of use and want, to which imperfectly we accomodate our lives, is a tangled and unbroken webb of institutions." Walton H. Hamilton, in *Encyclopaedia of Social Science,* VIII, 84. (The Macmillan Company 1933).

motivate policies of resource utilization. Such concepts are social in the sense that they cause individual objectives to be subordinated to the objectives of the group as a whole, although the group objective may be the well-being of its individual members. Among the almost limitless variety of objectives which human societies have at one time or another considered worth while are conquest and national glory, a luxurious life for an aristocracy, beautiful or lasting buildings or monuments, and a high and equal degree of material well-being and security for every individual.

Second, there are the prevailing or accepted *attitudes toward the proper methods* to be used in organizing the utilization of resources. These attitudes are reflected in the institutional framework of a society in which such important matters as the nature and extent of individual and collective control over the resources, the responsibility for their combination and use, and the division of the claims on the output are determined.

Third, there are the *natural* and *technological environments* which determine the character and quantities of those resources which are available for use and hence influence the kinds and quantities of goods that can be produced. The prevailing technology will also determine the manner in which resources can be most effectively combined for production—the use of steam power may require factories to be large or production to be large-scale.[8]

Since the accepted objectives, the attitudes toward institutions or social arrangements, and the available technology have continuously changed throughout human history, economic orders have always been in a state of flux—always evolving into something different, sometimes slowly, sometimes rapidly. In recent decades all of these factors appear particularly dynamic. So rapidly have economic orders been changing that it seems

[8] "Functionally cultural improvements may be divided into two groups: tangible changes of the natural environment such as canals, railroads, power houses, machines, churches, etc., which may be called artifacts; and, second, intangible cultural changes such as techniques, knowledges, acquired skill, etc., . . . Resource appraisal, besides being affected by changing wants and social objectives, ultimately depends upon the state of the arts [intangible elements of culture] rather than the supply of artifacts." E. W. Zimmermann, *World Resources and Industries*, p. 24. (Harper and Brothers, 1933).

sensible to cast the theory of social economics in resource utilization into a mould which is independent of any particular system of organization in so far as that is possible.

ASSUMPTIONS

The basic principle of economy in resource utilization is that the natural and technological environments shall make the greatest possible contribution to the attainment of social objectives.[9] Consequently, it is necessary to assume a particular set of social objectives and a particular natural and cultural environment before concepts of social effectiveness can be formulated, if they are to have any pertinency or usefulness. The laws for utilizing resources to obtain the greatest per capita output for a society would be of little use if that society were dominated by an aristocracy intent only upon increasing its own consumption of goods.[10] Likewise, there would be no point in analyzing the principles of advantage to be gained through territorial specialization for a society characterized by self-sufficient families.

In this exposition of social economics it is assumed that a primary goal of our age is the creation of a democratic society in which individuals shall have equal opportunity to develop and use their capacities and shall have equal access to the essentials for the good life.[11]

[9] A principle is here used to mean a fundamental, primary, or general truth, on which other truths depend. (It may also be used in economics as a rule or law exemplified in the working of a system; the method of formation, operation, or procedure exhibited in a given case; a fixed rule or adopted method as to action).

[10] Laws in economics are statements of the relations of certain phenomena in resource utilization, invariable under a given set of conditions.

[11] "Democracy. No definition of democracy can adequately comprise the vast history which the concept connotes. To some it is a form of government, to others a way of social life. Men have found its essence in the character of the electorate, the relation between government and the people, the absence of wide economic differences between citizens, the refusal to recognize privileges built on birth or wealth, race or creed. Inevitably it has changed its substance in terms of time and place. What has seemed democracy to a member of some ruling class has seemed to his poorer fellow citizen a narrow and indefensible oligarchy. Democracy has a context in every sphere of life; and in each of those spheres it raises its special problems which do not admit of satisfactory or universal generalization.

"The political aspect of democracy has the earliest roots in time. For the most part it remained a negative concept until the seventeenth century. Men protested against systems which upon one ground or another excluded

It is assumed that our society will continue to make use of machine technology, improving it as rapidly as possible so that needs may be more adequately filled. The multiplication of the effectiveness of human effort and the assimilation of the results of that increased effectiveness into the well-being of the members of society is economic progress.

Along with the assumptions of the desirability of a democratic society and the use of powered-machines to provide material well-being we must make a third—that the basic task of a society is to organize its economic activity so that the social aims will be achieved through whatever arrangements or institutions seem most effective.

Economics, then, is the science of the effective use of resources through social organization.[12] It is a study of the phenomena of resource utilization to the end that, through understanding and control, social effectiveness in the production, division and consumption of goods may be achieved.

---

them from a share in power. They were opposed to an oligarchy which exercised privileges confined to a narrow range of persons. They sought the extension of such privileges to more people on the ground that limitation was not justifiable. They felt and argued that exclusion from privilege was exclusion from benefit; and they claimed their equal share in its gains.

"That notion of equality points the way to the essence of the democratic idea—the effort of men to affirm their own essence and to remove all barriers to that affirmation. All differentials by which other men exercise authority or influence they do not themselves possess hinder their own self-realization. To give these differentials the protection of the legal order is to prevent the realization of the wishes and interests of the mass of men. The basis of democratic development is therefore the demand for equality, the demand that the system of power be erected upon the similarities and not the differences between men. Of the permanence of this demand there can be no doubt; at the very dawn of political science Aristotle insisted that its denial was the main cause of revolutions. Just as the history of the state can perhaps be most effectively written in terms of the expanding claims of the common man upon the results of its effort, so the development of the realization of equality is the clue to the problem of democracy." Harold J. Laski, "Democracy," *Encyclopaedia of the Social Sciences*, V, 76. (The Macmillan Company, 1933).

[12] Science here means accumulated and accepted knowledge systematized and formulated with reference to the discovery of general truths. Economics is the science of the discovery of truths that are helpful in organizing the use of resources.

Chapter I

Social Effectiveness in Resource Utilization

SCARCITY

"THE activity which brings into being new goods for the satisfaction of human needs is called production."[1] Unless such "activity" is carried on there will not be many goods available. In order to fill a large percentage of needs it is necessary either to reduce the volume of needs to merely enough goods to sustain life, or to maximize the volume of goods produced. It is inconceivable that today needs could be so reduced that some goods, at least, would not be scarce. Indeed recent generations have experienced rapidly expanding rather than diminishing needs as economic activity has become more effective through the use of scientific knowledge. Since the degree of scarcity is a consequence of the ratio between the volume of goods which resources produce and the volume of goods needed to provide for individual and collective well-being, scientific progress could make enormously greater quantities of goods available and yet scarcity would still increase if needs expanded at a greater rate than the volume of goods.

Certainly the fact of scarcity is obvious enough. Millions of people in even the most mechanized regions in the world do not get claims on sufficient goods to enable them to have the housing, food, clothing, health, recreation, education and security generally acknowledged to be essential to well-being. This state of affairs may be a result of one or more of the following conditions:

1. Human effort, using the other resources in the most effective manner known, may not be able to produce sufficient goods to provide well-being for every one.
2. Economic activity may not be as effectively organized for production as it could be with existing knowledge.
3. The claims on the goods produced may be so divided that many members of society get only a fraction of what is regarded as

[1] Gustav Cassel, *Theory of Social Economy*, p. 18.

essential for well-being, while a few get many times the requirements.[2]

The first cause of scarcity remains despite machine technology because the needed variety and volume of goods have increased as a result of population growth, higher standards of well-being, and the inclusion of all members of society among those whose well-being is to be enhanced. Furthermore, as more goods become available, more leisure from economic activity is needed to consume them. To produce more goods and still make possible adequate leisure for all will certainly continue to require the economizing of human and other scarce resources.

It may be that social arrangements permit resources to be withheld from use, or to be used ineffectively. Without doubt, the output of goods would be much greater if resources were as effectively utilized by human effort as the existing knowledge and techniques make possible. Mr. Stuart Chase, after careful consideration of the factors involved, estimates that the output of goods in the United States could now be about three times what it was in the pre-depression years.[3] In so far as this situation exists the scarcity of goods is due to those social arrangements which make possible an ineffective utilization of resources—arrangements, for example, which restrict the output of milk when relatively few children have the opportunity to consume as much as dietitians consider essential for proper physical development.

In any particular society scarcity for one individual or group may be due to the fact that others are permitted to lay claim to a large share of the goods produced. Farm tenants and industrial wage earners often live in dire poverty while the owners of land and produced resources live in great luxury.

SOCIAL EFFECTIVENESS

While conceptions of needs will vary with individuals and groups at a particular time and place, there are generally accepted social concepts of individual and collective needs and these concepts reflect the contemporary standards of well-being.

[2] A recent study indicates that the richest 36,000 families in the United States have a combined income equal to that of the poorest 11,500,000 families.
[3] *The Economy of Abundance,* p. 45.

Social effectiveness in production is inextricably bound up with social effectiveness in consumption and in the division of claims on goods (income). Consumption constitutes one of the primary aims of economic activity while the division of the claims on goods influences the nature of the goods produced and determines who will do the consuming. The attainment of social objectives will depend upon the coördination of the three phases of resource utilization—production, sharing, and consumption.

Many of the basic requirements for well-being are objective and measurable. They may be expressed in terms of the essential constituent elements of the diet, of housing, of clothing, of recreation and leisure, of education, and of economic security. They are determined according to the accepted techniques of the physical and social sciences, but are not absolute or unchangeable, for we are constantly acquiring additional knowledge of requirements for physical and mental health and new concepts of the good life. A very considerable variety within the constituent elements is possible. For example, the Bureau of Home Economics of the United States Department of Agriculture outlines food requirements for "our greatest national well-being" dividing foods broadly into twelve main groups: (1) bread, flour, cereals; (2) milk, or its equivalent; (3) potatoes, sweet potatoes; (4) dried beans, peas, nuts; (5) tomatoes, citrus fruits; (6) leafy green and yellow vegetables; (7) dried fruits; (8) other vegetables and fruits; (9) fats; (10) sugars; (11) lean meat, poultry, fish; (12) eggs. "Definite quantities of each are recommended . . . ; but the choice of individual foods within the groups is not limited . . . , so that the diets are adjustable to personal taste, prejudice, and food habits."[4] And while concepts of effective resource utilization may be stated in physical terms at any particular time, they rest basically upon generally accepted evaluations of what is and what is not worth the use of human effort and other resources—evaluations that are made intuitively.[5]

Although there will always be considerable difference in the

[4] See *Today*, August 18, 1934.

[5] "So far as empirical science can tell us anything about the matter, most of the proximate causes of belief, and all its ultimate causes, are non-rational in their character." (A. J. Balfour, *Foundation of Belief*, 1906, p. 399).

manner in which individuals use their opportunities to attain well-being, the attainment of social effectiveness in resource utilization does not mean giving to individuals what they think they want, or what they have been accustomed to have, or, indeed, what they may be able to obtain at a particular time under a particular set of arrangements. An individual's concept of his needs may be at variance with what is generally considered essential to well-being. Whenever such conflict occurs, individual objectives are subordinated to the objectives of the society as a whole. While it is the dominant social concepts of individual and collective needs that serve as the basis for whatever arrangements are used in organizing resource utilization, nevertheless the concepts may change more rapidly than the arrangements, thus creating a maladjustment between them.

Socially effective production makes needed goods as abundant as human effort, using the other available resources and working under satisfactory conditions, can make them. Scarcity is thus reduced to a minimum. Specifically the contribution of production to social well-being will be maximized when:

1. The largest possible volume of needed goods is made available for consumption.
2. Economic activity is itself carried on in such a manner as to promote the well-being both of the individuals engaged in it and of the society as a whole.
3. The goods which are produced are capable of promoting individual and collective well-being more than any other goods which could be produced with the same resources.

The sharing of the goods produced presents a two-fold problem. The manner in which the claims on the goods are divided among individuals and groups influences consumption and also, as a stimulus to individual activity, may considerably affect production. Therefore, a division of the goods produced will be harmonious with social objectives in production and consumption if it:

1. Provides the fullest possible opportunity for the good life making adequate provision for the physical, mental, and moral development of every one.
2. Encourages the most effective use of human and other resources, using variation in the volume of goods which workers may claim

only in so far as that would really be effective in increasing the output and in so far as it would not seriously conflict with other more important social objectives.
3. Provides for the use of goods through collective agencies (especially governments) whenever and to whatever extent such collective use will make the greatest contribution to the attainment of social objectives.

Resources are social assets and the basic economic problems are concerned with the attainment of effectiveness in their utilization, but the conditions just described as requisites are applicable only when it is assumed that all members of society are to be recipients of the opportunity to enjoy a satisfactory existence. Then there cannot be too many goods produced as long as there are individuals who do not have such opportunities. No society has yet produced too many goods.

ECONOMIC ACTIVITY

Economic activity is thus viewed as a means to an end; but since it requires so much of the time and energy of many individuals, it must also be regarded as an end in itself. It is bound to influence directly the individual's present and future position as a consumer and as a worker, as well as his enjoyment of his work.

One goal in organizing economic activity is to make it as beneficial and satisfying as possible to those who carry it on. It should not injure their health or deprive them of an opportunity for adequate leisure. Indeed the ideal situation would be one in which economic activity actually contributed to the physical, mental, and moral development and well-being of those who work. Each would do the kind of work he liked best and would put forth his honest and enthusiastic efforts. Such an ideal would be difficult to achieve in perfection in any society. Individuals react so differently to similar situations and they change their likes and dislikes as well as their capabilities in economic activity so frequently that there would necessarily have to be a continuous process of readjustment. Nevertheless, it is a goal which is in harmony with the objectives of a democracy.

To be most helpful in production an individual would engage in that activity for which he was best fitted and which provided for him the greatest possibility of developing whatever latent capacities he possessed; it would also be carried on under conditions which tended to induce his maximum effectiveness. The enthusiasm of individuals for economic effort and their willingness to coöperate is probably as important to the achievement of effectiveness in production as any other factor. It will depend not only upon the nature of the work itself but also upon the rewards for doing it and upon the conditions under which it is carried on. Rewards may be in the form of claims on goods, responsibility, or some sort of honors. Since individuals do not have exactly the same "nature," they do not respond alike to various inducements in economic activity, they do not all wish to do the same kind of work, and they are not equally well contented with the same working conditions. Yet it does not seem impossible to create working conditions which would approximate the ideal and at the same time maintain the discipline required for effective organization. Mankind, having had considerable experience in economic activity, has come to an almost universal condemnation of slavery because it breaks the "spirit" of the individual, reducing the output of goods as to little as the slaves dare produce. Of course, an economic order characterized by slavery was never intended to result in a maximum of well-being for the slaves. A wage system has replaced slavery of one sort or another, but it too may dampen the enthusiasm of many for the work they do if there is a feeling that the organization of economic activity does not conform to the accepted concepts of social justice. Wage earners may come to do grudgingly only what is necessary to retain employment.

Monotonous tasks, child labor, social injustice, unsanitary working conditions, ugly surroundings, excessive fatigue, meagre rewards, and slave-driving are all terms describing undesirable conditions for carrying on economic activity. Even though they are relative to ideals and do not have the same meaning to different generations or different individuals in the same generation, they nevertheless suggest the possibility of setting up standard conditions under which it might reasonably be expected that economic activity would promote individual and collective well-being.

Another contribution of working conditions to individual and collective well-being is security of employment. Idleness is a social waste of resources not only because it means a diminished quantity of goods for immediate consumption, but also because it may diminish the capacity or willingness of the unemployed to work in the future.

Finally, resource utilization can contribute to social well-being only if goods are produced which are more capable of promoting well-being than other goods which might have been produced with the same resources. It is frequently suggested that the making of luxury goods is beneficial to society because it gives resources employment; but other goods which would have made even greater contribution to social well-being could have been produced with the same resources. Recently there appeared in a magazine an article praising a large expenditure on the building and maintenance of a private yacht as beneficial to society. To produce and maintain this yacht more resources were required than are made available for the building and operation of many colleges. Every society must provide arrangements whereby resources are utilized to produce and maintain either such goods as yachts or such goods as colleges.

Chapter II

The Process of Resource Utilization

ECONOMIC UNITS

IN studying the various aspects of social effectiveness in production it is necessary to deal with the functions and interrelationships of the organizations designed to *control* the quantities, qualities, combination, and utilization of resources. By functions is meant purposes, tasks, or objectives. Such organizations are economic units—economic in the sense that through or within them resources are controlled in volume and type, and combined for production. They are organized for the purpose of providing, utilizing, and economizing resources and may be classified into three types according to the functions which are performed within them:

1. A socio-economic unit or social economy.
2. A production unit.
3. An industry.

The outstanding socio-economic units today are nations. They consist of interdependent and coöperating individuals and groups working toward common goals and governed in some degree by the same economic, social, and political arrangements. A national state is sovereign over most other institutions and arrangements which influence the well-being of the people as a whole. National policies determine the characteristics of the organization of economic activity within the nation, influencing the quantities and qualities of the resources available for utilization and the production, distribution, and consumption of goods and services. In some respects cities, regions, and even the world itself, are socio-economic units.

The actual production of goods necessitates organized units for the combination and management of resources. Farms, factories, banks, railroads, warehouses, steamships, highways, and the whole vast agglomeration of organizations in which there is separate, though perhaps integrated, management over the combination and utilization of resources, are production units. They individually make particular and definite contributions to the production of goods. One production unit may include all the resources used in making a particular good, but it is more likely to be one of a great many units which contribute to the production of one or more goods and hence a part of one or more industries.

AN INDUSTRY

An industry may include all of those production units which contribute to the output of a particular kind of article, making it available in the *form*, at the *time*, and at the *place* that it is needed. It is frequently convenient to narrow the concept of an industry to include only those production units which make the same sort of contribution to the production of goods.

FUNCTIONS OF ECONOMIC UNITS

The lines of demarcation cannot be distinctly drawn around these types of economic units but the concepts of them are useful, and indeed essential, in describing the basic functions which must be performed in any economic order. A socio-economic unit, such as the nation, must assume the task of providing a system of arrangements in which resources will be caused to exist in the most advantageous quantities and in which they will be utilized not only to produce as large a quantity of goods and services as is needed, if possible, but also to provide an institutional environment that will cause the production of those goods and services which will promote social well-being and their consumption by individuals whose well-being is to be enhanced. The basic function of the production unit is the combination of resources in such a manner as will be most effective in producing goods. The problem of organizing a coal mine, for example, is one of getting a combination of resources which will yield a ton of coal at the least resource cost, in order that as many resources as possible will remain available for the production of other goods. For an industry which is made up of many production units the basic function is one of getting the correct number of production units of the most effective size so that only as much coal, for example, as is needed will be produced in the most advantageous manner. Effectively organized production units and industries will maximize the output of needed goods in a socio-economic unit.

RESOURCE UNITS

Resources vary greatly as to characteristics and properties. Animate and inanimate "energy," skill, soils, minerals, forests, rivers, animals, buildings, and machines have but one common attribute—they aid man in the production of goods. Some of them have an additional common characteristic in that they are *scarce* and hence economized in an attempt to produce the most needed goods in the largest possible volume. To carry on this economizing of resources it is necessary to direct their flow into production so that only the correct number of units will be put in each of the various possible employments—a certain number of acres of land to cotton and a certain number to all other possible crops. An acre, being a specific area, is a land-resource-unit, but most acres are not similar except in area. They differ with respect to soil content, rainfall, days of sunlight, temperature, susceptibility to erosion or weeds, and the nature of the transportation facilities to centers of population. All of these factors influence the volume and kind of goods an acre of land would produce. The same is true of other resources such as men, mines, oil wells, factories, machines, a day's labor, and many others; they are classes of resource units but they are not uniform. Energy units such as horsepower and kilowatts may be very definite and uniform. However, *most types of resources may be subdivided into groups of units which are apparently uniform in their potential contribution to production*. Such a sub-division is essential because it is only by a comparison of the results of similar resource units in their possible uses that the most economical employment and combination of them can be achieved. A comparison of the probable results in using similar acres in cotton or tobacco production will make it possible to decide which crop to plant according to the relative importance of the two products.

THE ECONOMIC PROCESS

In every human society resources are in some manner controlled and directed into production by individuals acting for themselves or accepting responsibility as agents of other individuals and organized groups. The production units, which are organized to combine and utilize resources, may be isolated from the other resources to emphasize the nature of the economic process, even though as a part of the social organization they are themselves a cultural resource. The production process is a sort of circular flow of resources from the individuals and groups who have control over their utilization to the production units which actually combine and use them, and their return to the original source as the goods produced. The following diagram emphasizes this aspect of the process in a social economy:

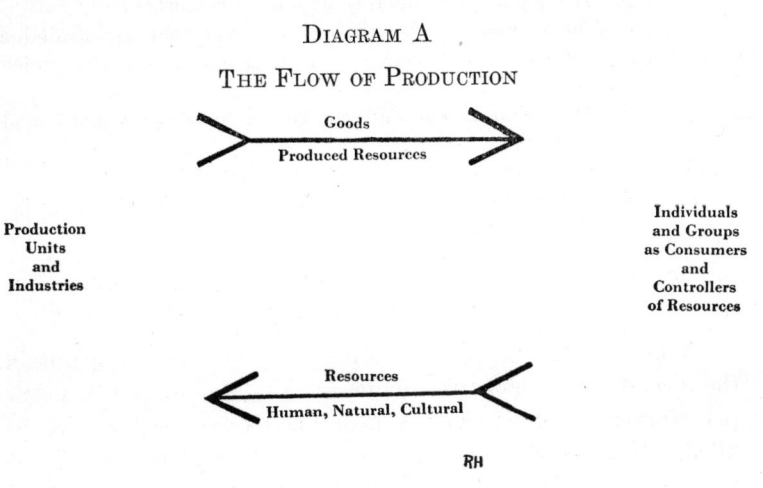

Diagram A
The Flow of Production

→ Goods / Produced Resources →

Production Units and Industries

Individuals and Groups as Consumers and Controllers of Resources

← Resources / Human, Natural, Cultural ←

RH

Certain commonplace observations about this economic process are pertinent to a further study of it.

1. The character and volume of goods produced depend upon:
    a. The character and volume of resources used in production, and
    b. The effectiveness with which resources are utilized by the production units and industries.
2. Many resources can be used to produce immediately either various kinds of additional resources or consumption goods. If more resources are produced the output of goods will not be as

large as it might have been for a time; but, of course, more mines, more machines, more factory buildings, more livestock, and other similar resources will increase the capacity to produce goods in the future.

Whatever goods are produced must be at the sacrifice of others which could have been produced with the same resources; the materials and human effort used in building the Empire State building cannot also be used to rebuild slum areas.

3. In whatever manner the claims on the goods produced are divided among individuals and groups, the total volume is fixed by the volume of goods produced. One generation may consume what a past generation has produced but the present generation may not consume what a future generation will produce.
4. Social arrangements and policies will influence the following:
   a. The nature and volume of the cultural resources accumulated as well as the manner of accumulating them.
   b. The quantity and quality of human resources.
   c. The volume of all existing resources that are available for use in production and the conditions under which they can be utilized.
   d. The organization and control of production units and industries.
   e. The kinds of goods that will be produced.
   f. The division of claims on the goods produced among individuals and groups.

CONDITIONS CONDUCIVE TO A LARGE OUTPUT PER WORKER IN A SOCIAL ECONOMY

A democratic society will attempt to create and maintain those conditions which are conducive to a large output of goods per worker in order that as many needs as possible may be filled. If wise social policies are to be formulated it will be necessary to thoroughly understand what these conditions are and why they are conducive to a large per worker output. The conditions themselves may be stated as generalizations or principles. For example, there will be a large output per worker in a social economy when—

1. The volume of natural and cultural resources is large relative to the number of workers.

2. The available resources are apportioned, combined, and utilized in the most effective manner possible.

THE VOLUME OF RESOURCES

The volume of human resources which will be employed in economic activity will depend upon the social policies regarding the work of men, women, children, and the aged, the hours of work per day and week and the work days per year, the physical stamina of the workers, their skill and effectiveness, and, finally, their willingness to work. The human resources that are to engage in production use the available tools, machines, processes, and various types of energy to change the raw materials of nature into goods for consumption.

The volume of other resources available to combine with human resources is limited by the quantity that is physically available, which sets the maximum, and by the existing set of social arrangements for their control. The volume of land available for agriculture in Great Britain, for example, is restricted by the use of large areas for hunting preserves. A socio-economic unit may try to plan the use of its natural resources in the interest of ordered development, and thereby restrict the volume of them available for particular uses, regulating the opening of new mines, new oil wells, and additional agricultural and forest lands for exploitation.

The volume of produced or man-made resources that are available depends upon social arrangements for causing their production, maintenance, and use. Sometimes, as in Ancient Greece, public buildings of great beauty and grandeur are more desired than additional ships or tools, which could have been produced. In other instances, as in Soviet Russia, a socio-economic unit will attempt for a time to divert nearly one-half of its resources to the making of aids in future production, such as machines, ships, mines, dams, railroads and buildings. At times, resources will be diverted to the making of additional resources for use outside of the nation, thereby causing their available volume to be smaller than it might have been within the nation itself. This latter was true in the case of Great Britain during the nineteenth century.

The influence of technology upon the volume of natural and produced resources cannot be over-emphasized. Natural resources which the past generation could not use at all are available for use today, simply because new techniques and processes have been discovered. Through some mechanical improvement a machine may be made much more effective in production than it formerly was, yet it may not require any more resource units to make the improved model than it took to make the old one.

The application of scientific knowledge to the arts of production has made the present day output of goods much greater than it has ever been before. Past civilizations might easily have accumulated the production equipment and furnished the human effort essential to the organization and operation of an economic system equal to ours if enough had been known about the properties of the natural elements and about mechanics.

Especially is the use of inanimate energy responsible for the present high degree of effectiveness in production. It is now possible to move great masses of materials long distances with little expenditure of human physical energy. High and low temperatures and enormous pressures can be kept under control. Hard materials can be cut with even harder ones especially prepared for the purpose. Substances, especially metals, can be fashioned with great precision. Stresses and strains in our tools, machines, buildings, ships, and bridges can now be measured and overcome. Mysterious agglomerations of electrons can be harnessed through the turning of dynamos by the pressure of steam, by the falling of water, or by the movement of tides. Through chemical energy and processes it is possible to build up soils and to break ores into their constituent elements—all this and much more through a knowledge of physics and chemistry. Such arts of production not only add to the "energy" at man's disposal, but they enable machines to perform tasks which throughout most human history have been done by the skilled and unskilled hands of men, women, and children.

But scientific knowledge and technique do not end with physics and chemistry and the inorganic sciences. Through the advance of the science of biology, and other sciences of organic growth, we have been able to improve the quality of livestock, grains, forests, fruits, and vegetables. Animal and vegetable products have become available in greater and greater abundance.

Furthermore, in the field of the social sciences we have learned something about the behavior of human beings and can, perhaps, construct the system of social arrangements in such a manner as to maximize the economic capacity of individuals and provide an environment in which they will willingly and enthusiastically coöperate in economic activity.

VARIATION IN RESOURCE VOLUMES

At any particular time an economic unit, such as a nation, an industry, or a farm, has a certain volume of resources available for combination in production—this volume depending upon their physical characteristics, upon the social arrangements under which they are to be utilized, and upon the scientific knowledge that can be applied in the production processes.

It is possible, however, to change the relative volumes of the various resources in the economic units. Over a period of time the population may increase or decrease, and the cultural resources may improve in volume and effectiveness or they may deteriorate. Many natural resources, however, remain relatively scarce. The volume and types of resources used in a production unit may be varied with even greater rapidity by shifting them from one use to another, though, of course, some resource units will be more difficult to shift than others and some cannot be shifted at all. Likewise, the volume and types of resources used in an industry may be varied over a period of time but the scarcity of certain natural resources will ultimately limit the degree of such variation as it does in the social economy.

Chapter III

The Law of Diminishing Returns

Variation in the Effectiveness of Human Effort

IF the workers of a social economy have a relatively large volume of natural and cultural resources to utilize, the output per worker will be relatively large. Possibly no better illustration of this principle can be found than in the influence of machinery on American agriculture.

Due to the use of machinery, the per-man productivity of American agriculture is so great and the claim of the agricultural population on the products of the soil is so small, that "the average American farmer (after allowing for the services of the hired laborer), in addition to feeding three other persons in his family, provides food and fibers for twelve people living in American cities, and elsewhere on farms, and for two more persons in foreign countries, a total of eighteen people." —"Few, if any, more farmers will be needed to produce twice or even three times as much farm produce than there are at present. . . ." "A hasty estimate indicates that the production of crops is about as great in North America as in Europe or Asia." But while the output is about the same in the three continents, there are only about 7,000,000 farmers in North America, as against tens of millions in Europe and perhaps hundreds of millions in Asia.[1]

From our general knowledge of the character and relative volumes of the different resources on the three continents we can conclude that scientific knowledge and its application to the agricultural arts exerts a tremendous influence on the effectiveness of human efforts, and that the relative volume of human and other resources is an influential factor in determining both the total and the per worker output.

Another illustration of variation in the effectiveness of human effort in different socio-economic groups is found in a comparison of quantities of goods that wages as a payment for human efforts will buy in some of the large cities of the western world.

[1] Zimmermann, *op. cit.*, p. 99. In this passage Dr. Zimmerman quotes O. E. Baker.

TABLE I

INDEX NUMBERS OF COMPARATIVE REAL WAGES IN VARIOUS CAPITAL CITIES*
LONDON = 100

	General Average Index Number Based on Food Only
Amsterdam	85
Berlin	63
Brussels	54
Christiana	80
Lisbon	29
London	100
Madrid	48
Milan	50
Ottowa	164
Paris	74
Philadelphia	221
Prague	57
Rome	48
Stockholm	80
Sydney	144
Vienna	46

* *Monthly Labor Review*, March, 1925, p. 53.

The workers in these capital cities do not have the same effectiveness in economic activity partly because they have not had similar training and partly because they do not have the same volume or types of resources with which to work. Furthermore, in exchanging the goods for food, the exchange ratio will depend upon the effectiveness of the rural peoples in producing food. In Philadelphia, for example, wages buy more food than in other cities of the world because human effort is relatively more effective in producing goods in both rural and urban industries. This situation suggests also the influence on the per person output of the volume of natural and cultural resources relative to the population.

The figures in Table I can hardly be more than rough estimates, especially since the different foods bought and consumed in the various cities are really comparable only with respect to those of their intrinsic properties which are essential in the human diet.

Such variation in wages measured in terms of food may not reflect material and non-material well-being because educational opportunities, provision for adequate housing, economic security and many other factors would have to be considered before the relative well-being of the wage-earners in these cities could be measured. However, the variation is so great that differences in the volume of resources relative to the number of workers are undoubtedly reflected in it.

It seems obvious that there is a physical limit to the extent to which resources can be utilized to increase the output of goods. To further illustrate this principle a comparison of the density of population with the yield of wheat in various parts of the world is helpful.

TABLE II

YIELDS OF WHEAT AND POPULATION DENSITY*

Region	Yields in Quintals per Hectare (1923-27 Average)	Number of Persons per Sq. Kilometer (1931)
Germany	18.4	139.0
Belgium	26.2	268.0
Great Britain	22.0	193.9
United States	9.7	15.8
Argentina	8.6	4.2
Canada	12.3	1.1

* Quintal = 100 pounds
Hectare = 2.471 acres
Kilometer = 3,280.8 feet

Evidently those regions which try to get more wheat to feed the dense populations can do so, but the yield of wheat per hectare is not increased in proportion to the density of the population.

Of course it is not to be inferred that the various socio-economic units utilize the land in the same manner—the number of acres of wheat planted per person differs and the methods and techniques used in cultivation also vary. The table does show, however, that for one reason or another, the yield per acre does not increase in the same proportion as the population. It may be that some have high yields per acre because they use only the most fertile land for wheat growing, having other more effective uses for the remainder of their land; it may be that the accumulated cultural resources of a particular region make its human effort more effective in producing things other than wheat. In any case, circumstances will prevent almost every region from producing exactly the amount of wheat it consumes and also will prevent each from having exactly the same yield per acre.

DIMINISHING RETURNS

What happens is that everywhere a more intensive cultivation of the land, by using more labor in preparing the soil and in cultivation and harvesting, fails to result in an increase in the yield as great as the increase in the volume of labor used. The same consequences would occur if the yield were increased by the use of more machinery or more fertilizer. There is a physical limit to the possible depth of plowing and to the additional quantity of the elements of the soil which deeper plowing makes available; there is a physical limit to the number of wheat plants that can grow on a given area and to the quantity of the soil which the plants can use. These physical limitations operate to cause a phenomena known in economic theory as diminishing returns. It is generally referred to as a law. This means that it occurs universally under a given set of conditions. Concisely stated the law of diminishing returns is as follows:

When a particular group of resource units is utilized more and more intensively by having additional units of other resources combined with it for production, a point is always reached past which the average output per unit of the resource that is added will decline.

The particular group of resource units to which other resources are added in combination for production may be the land of a country, the land of a region, the farm land of a group of farmers, or a single farm; it may be the production equipment of a country, a region, an industry, a factory or farm or a single machine; it may be the labor of a country, a region, a particular group of workers or a single individual. Although our present objective is to illustrate the operation of this law in order to show why a large volume of natural and cultural resources relative to the number of workers is conducive to a large output per worker in a socio-economic unit, the description in Table III is applicable in its operation to production units and industries as well. This table is constructed to show the consequences of varying the number of certain resource units in combination with others which do not vary in volume.

TABLE III
DIMINISHING RETURNS AND IMPUTATION IN RESOURCE COMBINATION

Combination of Resource Units	1 Units of Fixed Resource Fs	2 Units of Variable Resource Vs	3 Units of Physical Output Rs	4 Rs per V ARV	5 Rs per F ARF	6 Added Rs per V MPV	7 Rs Attributed to Vs IPVs	8 to Fs IPFs
1	20	5	115	23	5.7	..	..	...
2 IR	20	6	162	27	8.1	47	282	—120
3	20	7	196	28	9.8	34	238	—42
4	20	8	224	28	11.2	28	224	000
5	20	9	243	27	12.2	19	171	72
6 DR	20	10	250	25	12.5	7	70	180
7	20	11	253	23	12.65	3	33	220
8	20	12	253	21	12.65	0	000	253
9 DTR	20	13	252	19	12.6	-1	—13	265

TERMINOLOGY

Combination of Resource Units—This refers to the organization and utilization of resources through the economic units—nations, industries and production units.

F's—They represent a group of similarly effective resource units which are considered definitely fixed in number, for a time at least. Such a group may consist of particular human, natural or cultural resources in a nation or region, in an industry or in a production unit. With this definitely fixed group other resource units are combined in varying quantities.

V's—These are groups of similarly effective resource units which are made available in varying quantities for combination with the F's in economic units. In a nation, region, industry or production unit one group of resource units may increase while the others remain fixed—the population of a nation might grow, the factories of an industry or the machines in a factory might be enlarged in number. The possible quantitative combinations of the various types of resource units is unlimited. Within a short period of time it may be physically impossible to increase some of the types but over a period of time most of them, except the natural resources, can be varied.

R's—They represent the physical units of output—tons, bushels, square yards, pounds, and other units of physical measurement used according to the type of product.

ARV—The Average Return per unit of Variable resource is obtained through dividing the total R's by the number of V's for each combination.

ARF—The Average Return per unit of Fixed resource is obtained by dividing the number of fixed resource units into the total R's at each combination.

MPV—The Marginal Product per added Variable resource unit is found by subtracting the total R's obtained in the previous combination from the total R's obtained after adding an additional variable resource unit.

IPV's—The Imputed Product of the V's is found by multiplying the marginal product at any combination by the total number of V's used. This part of the total R's is imputed or attributed to the V's on the assumption that they are all alike in effectiveness in production and to each can be attributed what the last to be utilized adds to the total R's.

IPF's—The Imputed Product of the F's is found by subtracting the R's attributed to the V's from the total R's at each combination.

The Point of Diminishing Additional Returns is reached when a unit of variable resource fails to add as many R's to the total as its predecessor.

The Point of Diminishing Average Returns per unit of variable resource is reached when the number of R's added by an additional variable resource unit is just equal to the average for all the V's at that combination. Whenever an additional V fails to add as much as the average, then the average must begin to decline.

The Point of Diminishing Total Returns occurs when an additional unit of the variable resource actually causes a decrease in the total output of R's.

IR—This is the stage of Increasing average Returns per unit of the variable resource. The combinations in this stage are not economical for the average output per V could be increased by leaving some of the F's idle and combining the F's and V's in whatever proportion they occur at the point of diminishing average returns per V.

DR—This is the stage of Diminishing average Returns per V. If any resource is so abundant that it does not need to be economized it will be combined with scarce resources at the point of diminishing returns to them. All scarce groups of resource units are utilized into the stage of diminishing average returns to the other resource units, that is, they have imputed products.

DTR—The stage of Diminishing Total Returns is characterized by diminishing R's. Obviously no additional resource units would be added in combination which resulted in a smaller total output. If the V's are so abundant that they need not be economized they would be added only up to the point of diminishing total returns.

AS WORKERS INCREASE IN NUMBER

We have set out to explain why a relatively large volume of natural and cultural resources is conducive to a large output per worker. If we let the F's represent 20 million acres of land and the equipment for its utilization and the V's represent workers of similar effectiveness in economic activity, we can illustrate the consequences of combining a fixed volume of natural and cultural resources with varying numbers of workers.

As the number of workers increases from 5 to 8 million the total output increases at so rapid a rate that the average output per million workers increases from 23 to 28. This is the stage of increasing average returns to the V's and if there were only 5 million workers available it would be wise to leave some of the F's idle and combine the F's and V's in the ratio of 20 F's to 8 V's for then the average output per million workers would be 28 instead of 23. In the colonizing of any region such a plethora of land, forests and minerals actually exists that the colonists use only as much of them as will maximize the output per worker and leave the remainder idle.

After the fourth combination the average output per V

LAW OF DIMINISHING RETURNS 31

declines. At that combination the addition to output caused by the 8th V is just equal to the average output per V and the 9th V adds less than that average to the total so the average begins to decline. The fourth combination is therefore the point of diminishing average returns to the V's when there are but 20 F's available for utilization. This means that the *optimum* population of workers for 20 F's with the existing equipment would be 8 million. So a socio-economic unit might have too few workers considering the *potential* resources but after the point of diminishing returns to workers is reached the more workers there are, the smaller the average output of each becomes.

AS TECHNOLOGY IMPROVES

Improvement in the methods and techniques of resource utilization may affect the quality of resource units rather than the physical number of them. An improved locomotive may haul more ton-miles of freight per ton of coal used, the output of ton-miles of freight hauled being greater at all combinations. Such improvements may also change the point of diminishing returns to some resources or the rate at which the returns diminish. While improvements may seem to make the operation of diminishing returns unreal, since they cause an increase in the output of goods with somewhat the same physical resources, that is not the case. The locomotive may be improved but there are still limitations on the total volume of power it can develop and the number of loaded cars it can haul. As more and more coal is burned in a given period of time points will be reached at which the additional, average, and total horsepower per ton will decline respectively. Since improvements merely make the human effort of a social economy more effective in combination with the other resources, diminishing returns will be an important characteristic of economic activity until all needed goods can be secured without human effort.

If we assume that there does occur an increase in the volume of the natural and cultural resource units available we may use Table III to note the consequences. The 20 F's can now be made to represent a fixed number of workers and the V's to represent the natural and cultural resource units. Column*$ shows that

32   BASIC ECONOMICS

the average output per V decreases after the point of diminishing returns. Column 5 shows the average output per million workers and that increases up to the point of diminishing total returns. So the *optimum natural and cultural resource volume* is at the point of diminishing total returns to each type respectively. Only when more of such resources, if utilized, would actually diminish the total output would a social economy have too many of them.

DIMINISHING RETURNS AND THE RESOURCE-COST OF GOODS

Since the average output per F increases up to the point of diminishing total returns while the average output per unit of V decreases after the point of diminishing returns, it may be stated as a law that as the output is increased, within the stage of diminishing returns, the fixed-resource cost per unit of output declines while variable-resource cost increases. If the F's were workers, then added outputs as a result of an increased number of V's would mean a lower human effort cost per unit of output.

As long as there are unfilled needs there is no social justification for withholding resources from use if their use will add to the total output. There cannot be too much land or other natural resource or too large an accumulation of produced resources as long as additional units of them will cause human effort to be more effective. As those workers who engage in a particular economic activity are displaced by new machines or processes there is still no necessity for a lack of opportunity to work since many goods will still be scarce. Indeed social progress depends upon the assimilation of improved technology into production while all resources are kept fully utilized. Only then will the total output be maximized and the cost of goods in terms of human effort be minimized.

R'S IMPUTED TO V'S AND TO F'S

An interesting and important ramification of the operation of diminishing returns is the possible imputation or attribution of a part of the R's to the V's and a part of them to the F's. The explanation of the procedure for determining imputed products is simple, though in many actual situations the practical determination may be difficult if not impossible. It is necessary only to vary a situation by increasing or decreasing the variable resource, V, by one unit and then attribute the change in the output to the presence or absence of that unit. For example a weaver may be given an additional loom to "tend." The addition to the total output is then said to be "caused" by that loom. This is the so-called *marginal analysis* that is used to explain causal relationship in resource combination. In this illustration the last loom added is the marginal one and the additional output, caused by its use, is the marginal output of the total number of looms used.

Let us turn again to Table III for a numerical illustration of this principle. Since each unit of V is similar in economic effectiveness, the number of R's added by the last unit of V is said to be the imputed product of each V, and this additional output times the number of V's used gives the total number of R's that is attributed to them. Then the R's that are not attributed to the V's must be imputed to the F's, and this number is found by subtracting the total imputed product of the V's from the total R's at each combination.

As has already been noted the increase in R's added by the 8th V is 28, and by multiplying that number by 8 we get 224 which is the R's imputed to the V's. At this combination, which is the point of diminishing average returns, the entire output is attributed to the variable resource units. This situation is actually approached in a sparsely settled region where land is relatively so abundant that when all the workers are employed in utilizing it do not go beyond the point of diminishing physical returns to their labor. That is why the output per worker in such a region will be higher than in another region with a denser population, assuming the other resources to be equally abundant in both regions.

As additional millions of workers attempt to utilize the twenty millions of acres in our illustration, the average output of each (V) declines. The 9 V's, at the fifth combination, multiplied by the 19 R's added by the 9th V gives 171 or 72 less than the total number of R's produced. These 72 R's are attributed or imputed to the 20 F's.

At the seventh combination, with 11 V's, the total R's attributed to the V's is but 33 while the total attributed to the F's is 220. With the addition of the 12th V there is no increase in the R's, so all of them are attributed to the F's. The 13th V actually results in a decrease in the number of R's, and the point of diminishing total returns has been passed.

This analysis would be equally applicable if the F's were acres in a farm, the factories of an industry, machines in a factory or a group of workers, and the V's were units of another resource being combined for production.

POSSIBLE SIGNIFICANCE OF IMPUTATION IN A SOCIO-ECONOMIC UNIT

Imputation will occupy a place of great importance in a society which permits individuals and groups to lay direct claim to the imputed products of the various resources. Using our original illustration, in Table III, with F's representing millions of acres and the equipment for utilizing them, and the V's representing millions of workers, suppose that social arrangements permit one million of the workers to lay claim to the imputed product of the land and equipment. As the population increases the imputed share of the F's becomes larger while that of the V's actually diminishes. At the 7th combination we find 10 million workers getting only 30 R's while the one million who are owners as well as workers would get 223 R's. The rate at which returns diminish is rapid in this illustration and may tend to exaggerate the probable degree of inequality that may arise in the division of the goods produced under such social arrangements, but the principle involved is real enough. Perhaps that sort of situation will largely explain why people who own land, whether urban or rural, are glad to have the population grow while the American Federation of Labor favors a restriction of immigration.

It is significant that the average output per V declines slowly even though the additional output declines rapidly. An increasing density of population would not be so serious a social problem if the R's were divided equally as it would if they were divided according to imputed products.

The imputation process implies no ethical or moral claim on

the part of individuals or groups to share in the total output. Social arrangements determine who will be permitted to lay claim to the imputed products of the resources and they are subject to ethical and moral evaluations. Natural resources are the gift of nature and cultural resources are in large part an inheritance from past generations. Claims on them are permitted according to the contemporary ideas of social justice. Furthermore, *the imputed product of any particular group of resource units depends upon the volume and qualities of the other resources; all resource units help to produce goods and there is really no way to determine precisely what each contributes as a basis for immutable ethical claims on the output.*

IMPUTATION AND THE ALLOCATION OF RESOURCES TO PRODUCTION UNITS

The really important and practical use of imputation is in the allocation of the resource units between their possible uses in the production of various goods. When the ARV decreases it means that additional units of output cost more and more in terms of the variable resource units used. Suppose that the 20 F's in Table III are machines and that the V's are workers, the 10th V adding but 7 R's to the total. The practical question is whether or not the 10th worker might not produce more important goods at some other employment or, specifically, whether or not the 7 R's are equal in importance to other kinds of R's the worker might produce. This question must be answered with reasonable accuracy if resources are to be used effectively by those who control production units and industries.

In summary, while the use of imputation is very essential in organizing production, for it makes it possible to measure the relative importance of resource units in their various uses, it cannot be used with equal facility in dividing the goods for consumption because such a division might be quite contrary to the prevailing concepts of social justice and it might prevent the attainment of social well-being.

INFLUENCE OF TECHNOLOGY ON IMPUTED PRODUCTS

Improvement in technology means that more effective processes are known or better and more tools and machines are available for use. Such improved and increased cultural resources would utilize human effort farther into the stage of diminishing returns to themselves as well as increase the total output. The imputed product of human effort would therefore be increased and if the rate of diminishing returns to the cultural resources was rapid enough their imputed product might decline absolutely. In Table III the added R's per V do decline more rapidly than the V's increase and hence the number of R's attributed to the V's becomes absolutely smaller as more V's are added.

In so far as the improved technology enables the workers to utilize natural resources nearer the point of diminishing returns to their efforts, their imputed product will increase while that of the natural resources will diminish. So improvements in technology operate to diminish the marginal and perhaps the total imputed products of the natural and cultural resources.

OTHER IMPLICATIONS OF DIMINISHING RETURNS TO SOCIO-ECONOMIC UNITS

While it may be impossible to determine the optimum population either for the present or future, nevertheless the operation of diminishing returns in resource utilization is a basic consideration in determining policies affecting population growth, the accumulation of cultural resources, and trade in a social economy. Our illustrations have suggested the desirability of a society having a large volume of natural and cultural resources relative to the population. However, the returns to human efforts in utilizing other resources may be different for different individuals and groups because the resource units available to each of them may differ in nature and in relative quantity. If so, the total outputs of goods at the various resource combinations and the rates at which the returns to human effort diminish will differ among individuals and groups. In many instances the effectiveness of human effort in a social economy may be increased through specializing in the production of certain goods and exchanging some of them for other goods which can be produced with relatively less effectiveness.

Chapter IV

The Law of Comparative Advantage

SPECIALIZATION

THE operation of diminishing returns indicates the social advantage in a high ratio of natural and produced resources to the population. This might be called the principle of the best physical combination of relative total volumes of human and other resources in a socio-economic unit. An equally important principle of physical combination is that the various resource units should be so combined in the production of particular goods and services that the total physical output of goods will be maximized. This principle, stated simply, is that each resource unit should be put to that use for which it is best fitted and then used in the most effective combination with other resource units. The specialization of individuals and groups of individuals, by using other resources in the production of particular goods and services in excess of their own needs, increases the interdependence of persons and areas, necessitating the exchange of products between them. It is in this process of maximizing the results of human effort that natural and produced resources are put to specialized uses. Perhaps it will add to the clarity of our analysis if *specialization* is used to describe the committing of particular resource units to a certain use, for short or long periods, when there are other or more uses to which they might be put. Then the specialization of individuals and groups, including areas, can be described as a *division of labor*. This terminology serves to emphasize the desirability of combining natural and produced resources most effectively with human effort if a large physical output of goods is to be obtained.

CAUSES OF DIFFERENCES IN THE EFFECTIVENESS OF HUMAN EFFORT

Because of the availability of inanimate power and because of the simplification of tasks, the use of machines and other man-made resources is not only possible but necessary. Production has become indirect or roundabout in that resources are used in making more resources which are to be used eventually in the production of goods. This indirect method greatly increases the output of goods per worker because it enables the use of tools and machines. Machines, roads, mine shafts, canals, harbors that have been dredged, dams, railroads and many other produced resources are essential to the use of inanimate power. In the making of them it is obvious that a part of the resources of a social economy must be diverted from the making of consumers goods directly, but making possible a larger output of them in the future. A considerable part of the resources of any people who are advanced in scientific knowledge will be in the form of these produced aids and most of them will be of such a nature that they can be used only for certain purposes.

Even in the most primitive of human societies individuals develop special aptitudes for particular tasks and with the invention of tools the possibilities of special skills increases. With the advance of scientific knowledge and the technical arts, individuals must become more adept in certain activities than in others for the range of knowledge and skills is so great that an individual must be content to master only a particular field of knowledge or a particular skill. While the growth of scientific knowledge increases the differences between individuals in so far as technical knowledge is concerned, a great many skills, such as machine operation, may not be difficult to acquire.

It is readily apparent that individuals will differ in aptitudes, temperaments, skills, and experiences because of differences in biological and social inheritance. A broad classification of individual differences might be made as follows:

1. Physical—strength, endurance, skill;
2. Mental—knowledge acquired, ability to remember, analyze and classify;
3. Other qualities—capacity for leadership, willingness to make decisions and accept responsibility, ambition, moral stamina.

Whatever the origin of these differences they are factors which determine what sort of activity individuals are best fitted to carry on. To the extent that they are amenable to deliberate control, social effectiveness in production would be promoted through giving every individual the opportunity to acquire knowledge and to develop skills useful in economic activity. Since individuals not only do not have the same biological inheritance in some respects but it would be impossible for each one to acquire all knowledge or all the possible skills, a division of labor is necessary, and in so far as scientific knowledge makes it possible to discover what sorts of knowledge or skills individuals are best fitted to acquire, their effectiveness in economic activity may be increased by it.

Science has so increased our knowledge of the natural resources that more and more of them are made available and the properties of each type are being discovered, thus making it possible to use each one in the employment for which it is best fitted. A chemical analysis of the soil, for example, shows what it is best fitted to produce, as well as its deficiencies. The differences in the natural resources which make it desirable to utilize them in particular employments are easily explained. Soils differ in chemical content. Temperatures, rainfall, and humidity vary in the different areas. As a result grains, grasses, trees, and animals are better adapted to some areas than to others. Coal, petroleum, metallic ores, and building materials are found only in areas with a particular geological formation and history. Improvements in the means of transportation have made many resources available to all parts of the world. The basis for a division of labor between groups in different areas is apparent.

It would appear, therefore, that the advance of scientific knowledge makes possible and necessary a large quantity of produced resources designed to be used for specific purposes, it makes possible the discovery of what specific uses the units of particular natural resources are best fitted in production, and, finally, it causes individuals to develop certain aptitudes and capacities in addition to those biologically inherited. But these developments have not been and cannot be uniform with either individuals or groups.

DIVISION OF LABOR

Consequently individuals and groups differ among themselves with respect to the results of their respective economic activities because of variation in:

1. Personal aptitudes, skills, and techniques;
2. Types and qualities of resources available for utilization;
3. Relative volumes of the different resources available for utilization;
4. Degree of development in technology.

The basis for division of labor between them is the relative effectiveness of their respective efforts in producing two or more goods and services. When the efforts of one individual or group are more effective in producing a particular good than similar efforts of another individual or group an *absolute advantage* exists. Thus the people of the United States may specialize in the production of automobiles while the people of Brazil specialize in the production of coffee, as a result of an absolute advantage in each case.

A more complicated situation arises when individuals or groups can produce a variety of goods and services with the available resources but some do not have an absolute advantage in the production of any one commodity. The question of specialization becomes one of deciding what goods to emphasize in production. An answer to this question may be discovered through the operation of the *law of comparative advantage*.

COMPARATIVE ADVANTAGE

To illustrate this law let us compare the relative effectiveness of two individuals or groups, A and B, in producing two commodities (either in goods or resources), X and Y, in order to determine the conditions under which comparative advantage exists and consequently the conditions under which a division of labor will result in a larger physical output. The same principles would apply if the relative effectiveness of groups were compared, the groups being in the same community, in different communities, or in different nations. In these illustrations given quantities of each commodity are produced with six hours of similar human effort. The first case illustrates absolute advantage.

Case One

Commodity	Output of Each	
	A	B
X	30	10
Y	10	30

In this case it is quite clear that A should specialize in producing commodity X and B in producing commodity Y, for by each working 12 hours there will be 60 units of both commodities produced. A can trade 30 X to B for 30 Y and each have 30 units of both X and Y. In this case A has an absolute advantage in producing commodity X while B has an absolute advantage in producing Y.

However, if A were more effective in producing both commodities it may or may not be sensible for them to specialize. In the following cases there would be no point in either specializing:

Case Two

Commodity	Output of Each	
	A	B
X	30	20
Y	15	10

In this case with six hours of labor on each commodity either A or B can produce twice as many units of X as of Y. Neither would or could trade except on a basis more advantageous than 2 X for 1 Y, but that is the ratio at which both produce. Group A has an absolute advantage in the production of both commodities but neither has a comparative advantage.

However, if their respective outputs were as follows there would be a basis for trade and specialization, A having a comparative advantage in the production of commodity Y, and B in the production of commodity X:

Case Three

Commodity	Output of Each Individual		
	A	B	Total
X	30	28	58
Y	15	7	22

In this case it is obvious that 1 Y is *worth* 2 X in *labor-hours cost* to A while 1 Y is worth 4 X to B. If A could exchange 1

42   BASIC ECONOMICS

Y for 3 X it would be advantageous, for by specializing in Y production, whatever X was desired could be obtained with fewer labor-hours. If, likewise, B could exchange at a ratio of 1 Y for 3 X, that would also be advantageous, for by specializing in X whatever Y that was desired could be obtained for fewer labor-hours. The ratio of relative effectiveness in the production of Y as compared with X is higher for A than for B, and the ratio of relative effectiveness in the production of X as compared with Y is higher for B than for A. This means that the cost of Y in terms of X is less for A than for B and the cost of X in terms of Y is less for B than for A. The law of comparative advantage between individuals and groups of individuals in the production of various commodities may be stated as follows:

When the cost ratios, in terms of units of the human effort required to produce two or more commodities, differ between persons or groups, each person or group has a comparative advantage in the production of that commodity for which it has the relatively lowest cost ratio.

To illustrate the gains from specialization three different production policies may be assumed, using Case Three:

1. To produce the same amount of X, 58, and more Y.
2. To produce the same amount of Y, 22, and more X.
3. To produce more of both X and Y but in the ratio 58 to 22.

Let us take the first policy in which 58 X is to be produced and as many units of Y as is possible. If B specializes completely he will produce 56 X in 12 hours. If A produces 30 X in 6 hours he can produce 2 X in 24 minutes or two-fifths of an hour. That will leave eleven and three fifths hours to devote to the production of Y and in this time A can produce 29 Y. A will, therefore, exchange, 9.3 Y for 28 X. The result will be as follows:

	Total Output		Total each has after trade		Gain in
	X	Y	X	Y	Y
A	2	29	30	19.7	4.7
B	56	00	28	9.3	2.3

Let us now consider the second policy in which 22 Y is to be produced and as much X as is possible. To produce 22 Y, A would have to work 8.8 hours (twenty-two thirtieths of 12 hours). This would leave 3.2 hours to produce commodity X. In this time A could produce 16 X. B would produce 56 X in 12 hours. Trading at a 3 X for 1 Y ratio, the result of the specialization is as follows:

	Total Output		Total each has after trade		Gain in
	X	Y	X	Y	X
A	16	22	37	15	7
B	56	00	35	7	7

The third policy is somewhat more complicated in that we wish to increase both commodities as much as possible by specialization and in the ratio of 58 to 22. Again B will specialize completely in the production of commodity X and will produce 56 units. As stated above, A can produce 22 Y in 8.8 hours. This leaves 2 X to be produced by A to bring the commodity ratio of 58 to 22. The production of 2 X will require .4 of one hour. This leaves 2.8 hours in which A is to produce both X and Y in the proportion 58 to 22, and 2.8 hours is .233 of 12 hours. Let p equal the per cent of the 2.8 hours A will devote to the production of commodity X. We can then construct the following equation: 30p:15(.233-p)::58:22.

Using this algebraic equation we find that with the 2.8 hours which A will devote to the production of commodities X and Y, he will produce 7.9 X and 3 Y at the required ratio. The gain by specialization follows:

	Without specialization	With specialization	Gain
Output of X	58	65.9	7.9
Output of Y	22	25	3

How they will divide this gain will depend upon the bargaining or other arrangements between them, but at an exchange ratio of 3 X for 1 Y both will gain.

In this illustration, the differences in the outputs of group A and group B may be due to the differences in the skills of the individuals composing the groups themselves. If, however, they are in different regions and have different types and quantities of resources available to use in production, there would be a basis for specialization even though there were no differences in the individuals' skills. One group might have available an abundance of good wheat land but coal veins that were far underground and thin, while the other group might have available fairly good wheat lands also in addition to exceptionally available coal veins. Again one group might be using a different technology from the other, that is, it might have more scientific knowledge and relatively more man-made resources. A division of labor would therefore be as desirable between the people of different areas as between individuals of the same community; it is resorted to because the per capita output will be increased.

DIMINISHING RETURNS LIMITS DEGREE OF SPECIALIZATION

But there are certain human and physical limits to the extent to which the division of labor may be carried. The above illustration of groups A and B specializing in the production of commodities X and Y was over-simplified because the ratio of effectiveness in production was held constant even though the output was increased. Such a situation would not be typical because of the operation of diminishing returns. The comparative advantage of one group in the production of a particular commodity must be due to variation in the relative effectiveness of human effort in utilizing particular skills or fixed quantities of other resources. As either the human or other resources are utilized more and more intensively in resource combinations, each additional unit of output has a greater variable-resource-cost after the point of diminishing returns is reached. As group A specialized in commodity Y the operation of diminishing returns would sooner or later cause the ratio of effectiveness in producing X and Y to approach 3 to 1 instead of 4 to 1. This means that the comparative ratios of the resource cost of the various goods produced by different individuals and groups tend to become equalized through the operation of diminishing returns as specialization is carried farther and farther. Comparative advantage would, therefore, disappear as the ratios of effectiveness in producing additional units of the commodities became equalized. Due to these physical limits to which particular resource units can be utilized, few individuals and groups specialize completely.

While the division of labor makes possible an enlarged total physical output for all who participate in it, there is no tendency to equalize the per capita output between groups unless there is complete mobility of human resources between employments and areas. The goods available for consumption for both groups will be greater, but each will not have the same amount.

There are also psychological limits to specialization in that specific tasks may become uninteresting or monotonous if pursued for long hours each day or even over a period of time with short hours. Certain types of specialization might also undermine health.

CONDITIONS CAUSING COMPARATIVE ADVANTAGE ARE NOT PERMANENT

Only the differences in climatic conditions and other natural resources can be considered to have any permanency as a basis for the division of labor and even climate can be produced on a small scale and new processes may cause considerable increase in the availability of natural resources. Three outstanding conditions conducive to a division of labor are but temporary. They are:

1. Differences in the characteristics and in the relative volumes of human and other resources;

2. Relative differences in technology;

3. Differences in social arrangements which organize production of certain commodities through custom and through limitation of alternatives (e.g. share-cropper system.)

Of course it is always easier to increase the population than to decrease it, so an organization of economic activity based upon density of population may of necessity be fairly permanent, though it is likely to mean low per capita output. But the density of population in other regions may grow and any comparative advantage based upon it will disappear. The scientific knowledge and the produced resource of a region that is advanced in technology may find their way into other regions and thus destroy that basis for specialization. Likewise the abolition of slavery or a share-cropper system which holds a part of the population to a very low standard of living may remove a comparative advantage in the production of a commodity like cotton, for example; or the adoption of a similar or worse system in some other part of the world may give that region an equal advantage.

MEASURING THE LIMITS OF SPECIALIZATION AND COMBINATION

Vast improvements in the industrial and social arts have increased the production of goods per person because natural resources have been made more available, and produced resources have become more usable and more effective when combined with the human resources. Because of the resulting specialization it has become increasingly necessary to measure the relative social importance of goods and the relative effectiveness of resources in producing them. Inventions of technique in measurement enable us to determine what to produce and how to combine resources so as to get the most out of them. One of the most important inventions has been the use of money as a common denominator of measurement through pricing. Another is cost accounting, which has been invented to measure the money cost of goods to production units, and to determine the relative importance of units of the various resources in producing goods.

Chapter V

Least-Money-Cost Combination of Resources

NEEDED GOODS

WE have defined needed goods as those which will actually enhance what is currently considered social well-being, and we have pointed out that if production is to be socially effective it not only will make the largest possible physical volume of goods available but it will also make available those goods which will contribute more to social well-being than any other goods which could have been produced with the same resources. One of the basic economic problems is the determination of the kinds of goods that are to be produced and the quantity of each. Individuals and groups have various kinds of needs and various kinds of goods are required to fill them.

There are two limitations to the volume of a particular good that is needed. One is the physical limit to the capacity of individuals and groups to consume it; another lies in the relative importance of additional units of the various types of goods that can be produced with the same resources. As a particular type of consumption goods becomes available in larger and larger volume the added units are considered to diminish in importance. This may be called the law of the diminishing importance of additional units of a particular good. Since a social economy cannot approach the physical limits in the consumption of most goods because of scarcity, a choice between possible goods must be made. Consequently it becomes necessary to arrange the goods in the order of their importance to individuals and groups, causing only those types and amounts which have the relatively greatest importance to be produced. It is this "choosing" that determines the extent to which production will actually promote social well-being.

PURCHASING POWER

The claims on goods, expressed in terms of the money units which individuals and groups have at their command, constitute purchasing power or income. The division of these claims is a consequence of social arrangements but the total volume of goods that can be consumed is dependent upon the volume of resources used in the production process. A pricing process is essential to the organization of production and consumption but the importance of social arrangements in determining the volume of resources utilized, the division of the purchasing power among the members of society, and the types of goods produced, should be recognized if the social significance of prices is to be properly appreciated. Diagram B illustrates this aspect of pricing and also shows that it is the same purchasing power which arises from the use of resources that constitutes the claims on the goods produced, or, put in another way, the production of goods makes it possible to recognize claims on them.

Diagram B
Social Arrangements and Purchasing Power

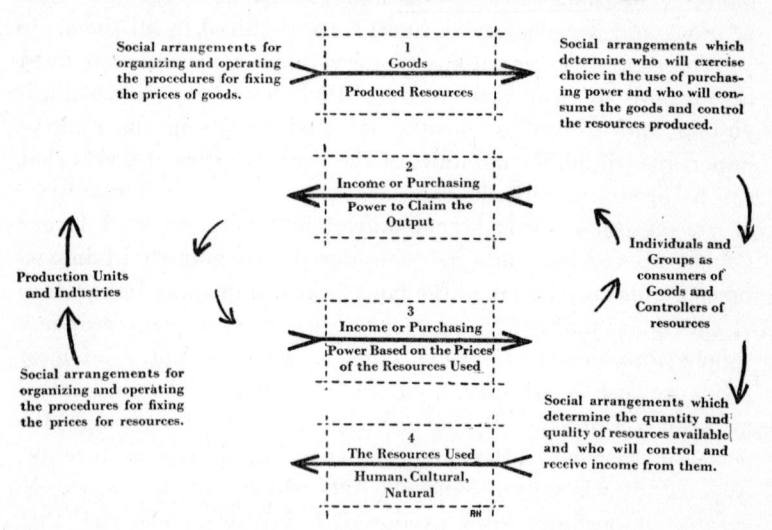

Social arrangements for organizing and operating the procedures for fixing the prices of goods.

1
Goods
Produced Resources

Social arrangements which determine who will exercise choice in the use of purchasing power and who will consume the goods and control the resources produced.

2
Income or Purchasing Power to Claim the Output

Production Units and Industries

Individuals and Groups as consumers of Goods and Controllers of resources

Social arrangements for organizing and operating the procedures for fixing the prices for resources.

3
Income or Purchasing Power Based on the Prices of the Resources Used

4
The Resources Used
Human, Cultural, Natural

Social arrangements which determine the quantity and quality of resources available and who will control and receive income from them.

Resource utilization is the source of the purchasing power which is available for use in claiming the goods flowing from production. If the effectiveness of the resources utilized is to be measured in money units, their total-money-price will have to equal the total-money-price of the goods which they produce.

All four of the rectangles in Diagram B would be equal if they are represented by money units.

Of course we are assuming a smooth flow of all available resources to the production units and of the goods produced to individuals and groups, thus balancing consumption and production of each commodity through the pricing process. If there occurred any inequality in the total volume of money claims on goods and the volume of money units at which the goods are priced there would have to be a shift in the prices of goods so that the purchasing power represented by the rectangles would become equalized. It might be possible to balance the purchasing power arising out of production for use in consumption by withholding some resources, or by encouraging the consumption of luxuries by a few, but the result would not be a maximum output of those goods which will most enhance social well-being. The goods which are claimed reflect only the choices of those to whom social arrangements give purchasing power; so, if those goods which will maximize well-being are to be produced, the purchasing power will have to be placed under the control of those who will make the necessary choices. The basic problem of the division of claims on the goods produced will have to be solved before social effectiveness in production can be achieved.

THE SOCIAL COST OF GOODS

Goods, obtained through economic activity to fill the needs of those individuals and groups who get control over purchasing power, have a social cost which is partly measurable in terms of the following:

1. Human cost—the time, health, energy, and general opportunity of individuals and groups to enjoy the good life.

2. Resource cost—the volume of the various types of resource units used.

3. Goods cost—The other goods which might have been produced with the same resources.

In order to minimize the social cost of goods it is not only necessary to produce in the most effective manner the goods that are socially most desirable but it is also necessary to carry on production so that it will be as beneficial and satisfying as possible to those who work.

The human cost of goods may be expressed in terms of the human efforts required to rear the children who become workers, in terms of the influence of economic activity on the health and on the future capacity for work, in terms of its influence in a worker's opportunity for the good life. Goods that are available for one generation have had considerable human cost to past generations which have accumulated the cultural resources used. Just as the concept of human cost is a product of the social concept of human needs, so also the actual human cost of goods is a product of social arrangements and attitudes. A society may or may not permit child labor, a long working day, and unsanitary working conditions in the organization of economic activity. Human costs cannot be measured in terms of money and if they could no useful purpose would be served.

The production of any unit of a good requires the utilization of a certain volume of resource units; its resource cost may be expressed in terms of the physical units of resources required to produce it. Of course, the human and cultural resources themselves have resource costs, so a unit of any particular good is a product of our whole cultural heritage.

Since social effectiveness in consumption requires that the goods which are most needed be produced, a very important item in the social cost of a particular commodity is goods which might have been produced with the same resources. It is a sort of opportunity cost, there being the opportunity to choose to produce some goods rather than others.

Now it is necessary, as we have suggested before, to find some method of measuring the relative social importance of the different goods that could be produced and also the relative importance of the various types of resource units in producing the goods. To enable such measurement these social costs must, therefore, be translated in some fashion into money costs. The relative volumes of the different types of goods that will be claimed at various prices will depend upon the choices of those who get the purchasing power. The costs at which different volumes of goods can be produced will depend upon the prices of the resource units. The prices of the resource units will depend upon the prices of all the goods which they help to produce and will determine the combinations in which they can be most effectively utilized by production units. Therefore, the social cost of goods can be measured, in part, in terms of money cost—though social arrangements will greatly influence the volume of resources available for use and the nature of the goods which are chosen for production.

THE IDEAL APPORTIONMENT OF RESOURCES

Our present task is to show why a correct-money-cost combination of resources is conducive to a large output of needed goods. We must take for granted in organizing and operating production units that the prices at which the different volumes of various goods will be claimed represent the relative importance of units of those goods in that particular society. At any given time there are definite quantities of the various groups of similarly effective resource units—individuals, acres, tons of coal, and countless others. What is essential to their correct apportionment is that each group shall be allocated to the various possible uses so that a single resource unit will not produce a more important output, measured in money units, if shifted to the production of another good. The correct apportionment of a particular group of resource units will depend, then, upon the relative prices of the various goods and the relative effectiveness of the resource units in producing the different kinds of goods. When additional units of a resource are used to increase the output of a particular good, the added units of output will be claimed for a certain number of dollars. A group of resource units should, therefore, be apportioned so that the last units utilized in each possible employment will have outputs that will bring the same number of dollars. The dollars which the output added by a particular resource unit brings may be called its money-product. The money-product which the last unit of a given group of resources will yield in any employment is the marginal-money-product of that group.

We will now illustrate this solution of the problem. Suppose that there are 20 million units of human effort to be utilized and that the alternative employments are grouped into five great classes of human needs. As each unit of human effort is added in combination with other resources in these employments, there is a decreasing number of physical units added to the total output of goods and as the output increases the relative importance of the additional units of goods declines to those who have purchasing power. Additional units of other goods become relatively more important because there is a physical limit to the quantity of particular goods that individuals and groups can consume and because there are various types of needs. Social arrangements will permit the payment of certain amounts of money for these additional units of output.

TABLE IV

MARGINAL MONEY PRODUCT OF 20 UNITS OF HUMAN EFFORT
USING OTHER RESOURCES

Food Money-Product	Clothing Money-Product	Shelter Money-Product	Education Money-Product	Recreation Money-Product
15	14	13	12	11
14	13	12	11	10
13	12	11	10	
12	11	10		
11	10			
10				

As more food, or any other good, is produced the additional units cost more in terms of human effort due to diminishing returns, and those who have purchasing power will not consider them of equal importance to the preceding additions. There will be a tendency, therefore, for the marginal-money-product of units of human effort to decline as more and more are apportioned to the production of a particular good. In this illustration more units of human effort are apportioned to food production than to recreation. That is primarily because the need for food of those who get purchasing power is relatively greater for it than for other goods, but it is limited by the physical, if not the psychological, capacity to consume the particular good. The increasing resource cost of additional units of food, due to the operation of diminishing returns, would also be an influential factor. Keeping in mind the operation of the law of the diminishing importance of additional units of a particular good and of the law of diminishing returns to additional resource units, the marginal-money-product of a given number of resource units will obviously depend upon two conditions: first, the amount of purchasing power which will be spent for different volumes of output of the goods they help to produce; and, second, upon the volume of the particular resource unit which is to be utilized—for the largeness or smallness of the volume would determine the extent to which diminishing returns would reduce the marginal physical output.

The ideal apportionment of the 20 units of human effort is attained when there is an equalization of the money-products of the last or marginal unit used in each possible employment. Exactly the same principle of apportionment is applicable to the allocation of other scarce resource units. Those resource units which are not scarce are utilized to the point of diminishing returns to the scarce ones.[1] Units of land available for either cotton or tobacco would be so apportioned between each crop that the marginal-money-product would be the same in each. Other resources flowing into use would also be allocated so that the marginal-money-products would be the same in all possible uses.

The actual attempt to approach this ideal is obviously reflected in the census statistics of occupations. The figures below show how the percentages of those gainfully employed in the different types of economic activity have shifted as a result of changes in the needs of consumers and in technology:

TABLE V

PERCENTAGE OF TOTAL GAINFULLY EMPLOYED ACCORDING TO OCCUPATION
1880-1910

	1880	1890	1900	1910
Agricultural pursuits	44.4	39.2	35.7	32.9
Professional service	3.5	4.0	4.3	4.8
Domestic and personal service	19.7	18.1	19.2	14.0
Trade and transportation	10.8	14.3	16.4	19.0
Manufacturing and mechanical pursuits	21.8	24.4	24.4	28.3

[1] Scarce in the sense that they have imputed products.

1910-1930

	1910	1920	1930
Agriculture	32.5	25.6	21.4
Forestry and fishing	0.6	0.6	0.5
Extraction of minerals	2.5	2.6	2.0
Manufacturing and mechanical	27.9	30.8	28.9
Transportation and communication	7.0	7.4	7.9
Trade	9.5	10.2	12.5
Public service (not elsewhere classified)	1.1	1.8	1.8
Professional service	4.5	5.2	6.7
Domestic and personal service	9.8	8.1	10.1
Clerical occupations	4.5	7.5	8.2

While this ideal is applicable to the allocation of all resources, the social purpose in production is to make human effort most effective. In order to maximize the returns to human effort it is necessary to utilize all other available resource units as long as additional units of them will add to the total output of goods. A correct apportionment of resources is achieved when the money-products of the marginal units are equalized in all employments; it is not achieved through maximizing the total-money-product of a group of resource units through withholding some of them from use. An over-simplified situation may be used to illustrate this point. Assume that 16 units of land are to be utilized in the production of four crops and that the money-products of each additional unit of land in the possible uses are as follows:

TABLE VI

Corn	Cotton	Tobacco	Root Crops
19	18	20	15
18	17	15	8
17	16	8	
16	15		
15	8		
8			

Under these conditions 16 units of land would have a total-imputed-money-product of $15 \times 16 = 240$, while 20 units of land would have a total-imputed-money-product of $20 \times 8 = 160$. A larger total money-product would be obtained if 4 units of land were left idle but it would mean a smaller output of goods available for consumption.

Human resources may, however, be withheld from use because the additional goods that might be produced are not considered as socially important as leisure or non-economic activity. The abolition of child labor and the shorter hours of work per day indicate a social emphasis upon leisure and opportunity for non-economic activity.

Circumstances which operate to withhold natural and produced resources from use work against the attainment of social effectiveness in production. During a period of breakdown in the coördination of a social economy, the idleness of resources results in a low per person output and it is necessary to forego the consumption of goods that would be available if they were not idle.

It is obvious that a correct apportionment of all available or usable resources will maximize the physical output of needed goods; but it must be constantly emphasized that if needs are measured through the use of purchasing power by those who have it, the existing social arrangements may permit such a division of claims on goods produced that social efficiency in consumption is not promoted by the production of certain goods, even though they are claimed. The obstacle to the attainment of social well-being does not lie in the use of prices to apportion resources but in the social arrangements which determine the division of claims on goods and the manner in which these claims are exercised to direct production.

THE INTERDEPENDENCE OF PRICES

We have stated, as a principle, that if resources are to be economized they must be utilized in producing the most needed goods in the most effective manner. It is necessary to measure the effectiveness of different resource combinations in the production units to accomplish effective utilization. Such measurement is possible only through a comparison of the money costs of various combinations, but resource units must be priced before money cost can be known.

We may summarize the principle of resource utilization just described and state a second, which is now to be analyzed, as follows:

1. The correct price of a particular group of similar resource units corresponds with the marginal-money-product of those units when such products are *equalized* in all employments, and when *all* of the available resource units are utilized. This marginal-money-product is dependent upon the prices of the products which the resource units aid in producing, while the prices at which various quantities of the different products will be claimed will depend upon the concepts of individual and group needs held by those who get control over the purchasing power and who can, therefore, direct the production of particular goods.

2. The correct combination of resources in production units is that which will result in the *least-money-cost* per unit of output. For an industry the correct combination and utilization would be one which would produce a total output that would be claimed (bought) at a price equal to the cost at the least-money-cost combination, while all the constituent production units were operating at that least-money-cost combination. The price of a particular good is, then, a consequence of the price of the resources utilized in producing it, and the prices of resource units reflect the prices of goods in general.

LEAST-MONEY-COST COMBINATION IN A PRODUCTION UNIT[2]

At any particular time the production units of an industry will have some resource units which cannot readily be increased in quantity, while others may easily be added in combination. To the managers of production units both the fixed and variable resource units have a cost presumably based upon their marginal-money-products in all uses. The least-cost combination will be located somewhere between the points of diminishing average and of diminishing total returns to the variable resource units, depending upon the relative costs of both fixed and variable resources. If the fixed resource has no cost at all then the least cost combination will be at the point of diminishing returns to the variable resource units, for that is the point of its highest average physical output per unit. If the variable resource has no cost, then the least-cost combination will be at the point of

---

[2] The term cost will be used to mean money cost unless specific exception is made.

diminishing total returns to it, for at that point the average output per unit of the fixed resource units would be maximized. Within the stage of diminishing returns to the variable resource units their cost per unit of output increases, while the cost of the fixed resource per unit of output decreases as more variable resource units are added. When the increase in the cost of the variable resource per unit of output is just offset by the decrease in the cost of the fixed resource, the average cost per unit of output will be lower than at any other combination; it will be the least-cost combination. As long as the decrease in the fixed cost is greater than the increase in the variable cost the average cost per unit of output will decline. When the increase in the variable cost becomes greater than the decrease in the fixed cost the average cost per unit of output will increase. Therefore if the variable resource units are relatively more expensive than the fixed resource units the operation of diminishing returns will cause the least-cost combination to be reached sooner than if the opposite situation existed.

These aspects of the least-money-cost combination may be made more realistic by a simple illustration of the production unit in the form of a fruit canning plant which operates a single "line" of coördinated machines of a particular size. As few as 10 men might operate the line, yet if the machinery is run at full speed and tasks sufficiently specialized as many as 110 may work without causing a decrease in the total output. The daily output varies with the number of men operating the production unit as follows:[3]

Number of Men	10	20	30	40	50	60	70	80	90	100	110	120
Output Hundreds of Cans	0.5	3.0	6.4	10.0	13.6	16.9	19.6	21.7	23.0	23.7	23.7	23.4
Average Output Per 10 Men	0.5	1.5	2.1	2.5	2.7	2.8	2.8	2.7	2.6	2.4	2.2	2.0

The most canned fruit per worker working is obtained with from 60 to 70 workers, that is to say, at the point of diminishing average returns; but the machines-line is also a resource made

[3] This illustration and the tables which are based upon it are adapted from *Production Organization* by J. D. Black and A. G. Black with the permission of the publisher, Henry Holt and Company (1929).

by man and has a price based upon the money-product of resources used in making machines in general and hence upon their money cost. Under these circumstances what is desired, if social effectiveness in production is to be achieved, is a combination which will give units of output for the least-total-resource cost, money being the common denominator of resource measurement which makes it possible to determine the total resource cost of different volumes of output. To illustrate, we may assume that the machine-line of the fruit canning plant has a cost of $200 per day and that each worker has a cost of $4 per day. The total cost of the various combinations of workers with the machine line may now be found and if the output is divided into the total cost the result obtained will be the cost per hundred cans of fruit. That combination which gives the lowest cost per hundred will be the least-cost combination.

TABLE VII

LEAST-MONEY-COST COMBINATION

Worker	Line	Costs Workers at $4.00	Machine at $200	Total Money Costs	Total Output (in Hundreds)	Cost Per Hundred of Output
10	1	$ 40	$200	$240	0.5	$480.00
20	1	80	200	280	3.0	93.33
30	1	120	200	320	6.4	50.01
40	1	160	200	360	10.0	36.00
50	1	200	200	400	13.6	29.40
60	1	240	200	440	16.9	26.04
70	1	280	200	480	19.6	24.48
80	1	320	200	520	21.7	23.97
90	1	360	200	560	23.0	24.35
100	1	400	200	600	23.7	25.32
110	1	440	200	640	23.7	27.00
120	1	480	200	680	23.4	29.05

The influence of relative changes in the money cost of resource units is illustrated in Table VIII. It is obvious that as the machine-line becomes relatively lower in cost the least-cost combination approaches the point of diminishing returns and that as the workers become relatively low in cost, the least-cost combination approaches the point of diminishing total output.

TABLE VIII
LEAST-MONEY-COST COMBINATIONS

Combination of Workers	First Set of Cost Rates			Second Set of Cost Rates			Third Set of Cost Rates		
	Machine Line $200	Workers $4 each	Combined Cost Per 100 Cans	Machine Line $100	Workers $8 each	Combined Cost Per 100 Cans	Machine Line $300	Workers $2 each	Combined Cost Per 100 Cans
10	$400.00	$80.00	$480.00	$200.00	$160.00	$360.00	$600.00	$40.00	$640.00
20	66.66	26.67	93.33	33.33	53.34	86.67	99.99	13.33	113.32
30	31.26	18.75	50.01	15.63	37.50	53.13	46.89	9.38	56.27
40	20.00	16.00	36.00	10.00	32.00	42.00	30.00	8.00	38.00
50	14.70	14.70	29.40	7.35	29.41	36.76	22.05	7.35	29.40
60	11.84	14.20	26.04	5.92	28.40	34.32	17.76	7.10	24.86
70	10.20	14.28	24.48	5.10	28.57	*33.67*	15.30	7.14	22.44
80	9.22	14.75	*23.97*	4.61	29.50	34.11	13.83	7.37	21.20
90	8.70	15.65	24.35	4.35	31.30	35.65	13.05	7.83	*20.88*
100	8.44	16.88	25.32	4.22	33.75	37.97	12.66	8.44	21.10
110	8.44	18.56	27.00	4.22	37.13	41.35	12.66	9.28	21.94
120	8.54	20.51	29.05	4.27	41.02	45.29	12.81	10.26	23.07

It is significant that the costs of the machine-line per 100 cans of output diminishes as long as the total output increases. Since the total fixed or "overhead" resource cost does not fluctuate with the output, a larger output means a lower average fixed-resource-cost. After the point of diminishing physical returns to the variable resource units (workers in this case) is reached, additional units of output cost more in terms of the variable resource. Therefore to repeat, as the output increases within the stage of diminishing returns, the money cost of the fixed resource units decreases while the money cost of the variable resource unit increases. When the decreased money cost of the machine-line per unit of output is just equal to the increase in the money cost of workers per unit of output, the least-money-cost combination will have been reached. For example, in Table VII when the number of workers is increased from 70 to 80 the money cost of the machine-line per hundred cans decreases from 10.20 to 9.22 or .98 while the worker cost per hundred cans increases from 14.28 to 14.75 or .47, but when the number of workers in increased from 80 to 90 the machine line cost per hundred cans decreases from 9.22 to 8.70 or .52 while the worker cost increases from 14.75 to 15.65 or .90. If the decrease in the cost of machine-line per hundred cans fails to offset the increase in the cost of the workers, additional units of output will have an increasing-average-money-cost.

LEAST-MONEY-COST COMBINATION AND SOCIAL EFFECTIVENESS IN PRODUCTION

It is at this least-money-cost combination that the volume of resources required to produce a unit of output is minimized. But over a period of time it is possible to change the volume and character of the "fixed" resource units—in fact, all the resources are variable for most production units if sufficient time is allowed for the physical task of changing their combination. Consequently the concept of social effectiveness in production, involving the maximization of the physical output per worker in the social economy, has far greater implications than are suggested in the fruit canning plant illustration. Over a period of time the building might be enlarged and a new and improved machine-line might be installed. Social effectiveness in the fruit canning plant, as in any production unit, requires that it make use of the most effective technology as well as operate at the least-money-cost combination.

THE CONCEPT OF LEAST-MONEY-COST IN AN INDUSTRY

An industry will be organized with maximum social effectiveness when the correct number of production units are in operation and each one has the best possible resource combination. Each production unit would then have the same cost per unit of output.

The concept of the correct number of production units for an industry is very important. It is based primarily on the concept of the correct apportionment of resource units to their various possible employments—a correct apportionment being achieved when the marginal products are equalized for each employment. A correct apportionment of resources between employments, along with their use in a least-cost combination simply means that an industry would have operating at the least-cost combination that number of production units whose total output would be claimed at a price equal to the cost. In the fruit canning plant ilustration, the price per 100 cans would be equal to the least-money-cost and the industry would have as many such production units as would produce a total output which those with purchasing power will claim.

However, in an industry as in a production unit, certain dynamic factors make it difficult, from a physical standpoint, to organize and operate exactly the correct number of production units at the most effective resource combination possible.

DYNAMIC FACTORS IN THE PRODUCTION PROCESS

In all human societies there appears to be constant change in the types of goods needed and in their relative importance. Consequently the volumes of the various goods that will be claimed at different prices are in a more or less constant state of flux. Situations arise which make it necessary to increase the number of production units in some industries, decrease them in others, and also to organize completely new industries.

There appears, also, to be continual improvement in technology through scientific progress, especially in societies using powered machines. As Walter Lippman puts it: "We have invented invention." The result of such improvements is to increase outputs in the various resource combinations, lower the cost at the most effective combination, and necessitate the repricing of many, if not all, of the resource units.

Then, too, it is impossible to duplicate exactly the human resources in the various production units and industries in the way that machines, buildings, and processes can be duplicated. Because of the differences in individuals and in the same individuals at different times, it is too much to expect that exactly the same methods can be used in all similar production units or the same results secured.

LEAST-MONEY-COST AND CHANGING NEEDS

When a larger volume of output is needed than an industry can produce with the existing production units operating at the least-cost combination, it will be necessary to operate beyond that combination. The additional units of output can be produced only at a greater resource and hence a greater money cost. In the fruit canning plant the average cost of the additional units of output is as follows:

TABLE IX

THE MONEY-COST OF ADDITIONAL OUTPUTS

Number of Workers	Additional Outputs (100 cans) Per Day	Cost of Added Workers at $4 Per Day	Average Additional Cost	Average Total Cost
10	0.5	$40	$80	$480
20	2.5	40	16	93.33
30	3.4	40	11.76	50.01
40	3.6	40	11.11	36.00
50	3.6	40	11.11	29.40
60	3.3	40	12.12	26.04
70	2.7	40	14.82	24.48
80	2.1	40	19.05	23.97
90	1.3	40	30.77	24.35
100	0.7	40	57.14	25.32
110	0.0	40	....	27.00
120	—0.3	40	....	29.05

When production is carried past the least-cost combination the cost of the additional units of output is greater than the average total cost at the least-cost combination. When production is carried beyond that combination it is an evidence that both the fixed and variable resource units are not being used in adequate quantities in the industry; in other words, there should be more production units, considering the need for the goods produced.

In the expansion of an industry through the multiplication of production units, it is frequently impossible to obtain more of certain resource units of the same type or quality. An increased output can be obtained then only by using the fixed resources more intensively (farther into the stage of diminishing returns to the variable resource units) or by using other available resource units of a lower quality. Sometimes an industry is not able to obtain resources for expansion except by shifting them away from other industries and this results in a higher marginal-money-product and hence a higher price. For example, if we attempt to increase our output of anthracite coal either the existing mines will have to be worked more intensively or new and perhaps less effective shafts will have to be opened. And perhaps it will be necessary to shift some miners from the bituminous fields, the need for whose product has not diminished, thus causing a repricing of the worker's efforts to a higher level. In any case, the additional units of output would be secured only at a higher-least-cost combination. The imputed-money-product of the old and more effective mines would also be increased as they are utilized farther into the stage of diminishing returns to the variable resource units.

If the situation is reversed and the output of an industry is not claimed at a price equal to the least-cost combination, it means that there are too many production units in the industry. Two results should follow. Those resource units which can be, should be shifted to other employments until their marginal-money-products in all uses are equalized; this will reduce somewhat the total output of the over-expanded industry. But those resource units which cannot be shifted must be repriced and the price of the goods decreased until the total output of the industry will be claimed. Social effectiveness in production requires the use of all available resource units regardless of what happens to their imputed-money-products.

Sometimes, as in the case of a railroad, it is necessary to commit large volumes of resources to forms that can be used only for one purpose. Once this is done social effectiveness in production would require that variable resources, such as workers, should be added in the operation of the fixed resources as long as their marginal-money-product is as great as in other uses, regardless of whether or not the fixed resources have any imputed-money-product.

LEAST-MONEY-COST AND SCIENTIFIC PROGRESS

Scientific progress means that human effort is made more effective in obtaining needed goods from the other available resources. In certain instances it will mean that the relative effectiveness of many resource units committed to particular use will be less, and they will have a decreased marginal money product. In other instances it will mean that a relatively larger volume of particular resources are available and will thus lower the marginal money product of the units of the group. The advance of scientific agriculture will result in a decline in the money product of land resources. Scientific progress is then likely to require the constant and extensive repricing downward of resources which have been made obsolete, more effective, or available in greater volume.

LEAST-MONEY-COST IN A SOCIO-ECONOMIC UNIT

Because of the existence of comparative advantage between individuals, communities, regions, nations, and continents, a division of labor will, as we have shown, increase the total output of goods. Since these individuals and groups differ in personal aptitudes, skills, and techniques, in the types, qualities and relative volumes of the resources available for utilization, and in the degree of development in technology, there will occur differences in the prices of some resources, especially those which are not shiftable between areas. Hence in the case of an absolute advantage, least-money-cost combinations will be different since some regions cannot produce certain goods at all. But where there is a comparative and not an absolute advantage the least-money-cost combinations are likely to be the same in all socio-economic units, but specialization between them will take place before the money costs are equalized. In any case the only difference in the prices and in the cost of goods in the various groups, wheat for example, will be mainly that of transportation cost if exchange takes place. Through such division of labor, socio-economic units maximize the physical output of goods because they are able to specialize in the production of those goods which can be produced with the least-resource-cost.

SUMMARY OF THE PRINCIPLES OF SOCIAL ECONOMICS IN RESOURCE UTILIZATION

Resources, being those elements of the environment which contribute toward the filling of needs, are economized by obtaining as large a volume of goods as possible from their utilization. Economizing is desirable because many needs remain unfilled in all generations. In the process of economizing them the basic problems are—How to get the maximum volume of goods to be obtained? What goods are most important? and Who shall consume them? Resource utilization is carried on through the social arrangements which constitute the economic order. Social objectives, social attitudes, and the natural and technological environments determine the nature and characteristics of an economic order.

In the analysis of the principles of social economics it was assumed that the predominant social objective was the creation of a democratic society with a high level of material well-being. It was further assumed that it would continue to use the most advanced technology possible, through whatever sort of economic order would be most effective.

A scarcity of goods exists when they are insufficient in volume to meet the needs of a society. It may be caused by needs being greater than human effort, the most effective technology, can fill; by the failure of a society to effectively organize production; or by the goods that are produced being so divided among the members of a group that the socially most pressing needs are not filled. It is likely to be a result of all these conditions.

The concept of social effectiveness in resource utilization is reflected in the generally accepted requirements for the good life, expressed in terms of housing, food, clothing, recreation and leisure, education and security.

Social effectiveness in production and consumption is achieved when the largest possible volume of the socially most needed goods are made available through economic activity that, in itself, promotes the well-being of those who work, and gives proper consideration to the resource needs of future generations.

Social effectiveness in the division of goods and in consumption is achieved when the highest possible level of living is made available for all, when adequate provision is made for the mental, physical, and moral development of every individual, when the most effective use of resources is encouraged, and when collective consumption is extended whenever it will contribute more to the attainment of social objectives than individual consumption.

Resource utilization is carried on through organized units which may be classified as socio-economic, production and industrial units. While the lines of demarcation cannot be distinctly drawn between them, their essential functions are to provide the social arrangements and the technician organization which will enable the production of the socially most needed goods.

Resources must themselves be classified and broken up into units so that their relative effectiveness in various uses may be measured.

In the process of utilizing resources, units of them flow into production, resulting in an output of needed goods which in turn flow into consumption. The volume of the goods output will depend upon the volume and effectiveness of the resources used, and the nature and use of the goods produced will depend upon the social arrangements which provide for their division and consumption.

A large volume of natural and cultural resources relative to the number of workers and a correct apportionment combination and utilization of the resources in production are conducive to a large output of needed goods per worker.

A small volume of workers relative to the volume of natural and cultural resources is conducive to a large per capita output because the operation of diminishing returns causes the output per worker to decrease as their number grows, after the point of diminishing returns (to workers) has been reached. Within the stage of diminishing returns the variable resource cost of additional units of output in the production units increases and hence imputation is an important part of the analysis of the effective apportionment and combination of resource. The imputation of the output to the various resource units utilized in its production cannot, however, be used as a basis for dividing up the goods produced among the members of a democratic society for consumption.

A correct physical combination of resources is conducive to a large output per worker because it enables specialization, which means that resource units are used in those employments in which they are relatively most effective. A division of labor between individuals and groups, based upon differences in the natural, human, and cultural resources which create a comparative advantage for particular individuals and groups in the production of certain goods, increases the total volume of goods available for all.

Cost may be expressed in terms of the human consequences, in terms of the physical volumes of the resources used, or in terms of the goods which might have been produced with the same resources. The effective apportionment and combination of resource units requires that the relative importance of goods and the relative effectiveness of resource units in producing goods be measured. A comomn denominator of comparison is used for this purpose. It is called money.

Money units are used to measure the relative social importance of goods and the relative effectiveness of resource units as aids in production. Units of goods and of resources are therefore priced in terms of money units. A least-money-cost combination in a production unit means that the output of goods per unit of combined resources used is being maximized. A least-money-cost for an industry means that the resources are being apportioned through specialization and combined into production units to produce the correct total volume of each of the different goods. A least-money-cost for production in a social economy means that proper consideration is being given to comparative advantage between communities, regions, and nations, and the physical volume of goods for consumption is being maximized through a division of labor; it means that production units and industries combine and use resources so as to obtain the largest volume of needed goods in so far as the division of purchasing power permits.

PART II. FUNCTIONS IN RESOURCE UTILIZATION

INTRODUCTION

FUNCTIONS TO BE PERFORMED

FUNCTIONS AND THE BASIC ECONOMIC PROBLEMS

EVERY human society develops social arrangements of some sort which are designed to influence the relative volume in which the various resources will be available for utilization, to combine the resource units in production, to determine the kinds and volumes of goods that are to be produced, and to select the individuals and groups who are to consume them. The development of such important arrangements is itself an essential function of a social economy. Their nature will be determined, as we have previously suggested, by the prevailing social objectives, social attitudes, and the natural and technological environments. We are not, however, at present concerned with the almost limitless variety of these social arrangements which might constitute an economic order. We are interested, rather, in the essential functions or tasks which must be performed if a democratic society using a machine technology is to achieve an effective utilization of resources.[1] They are essentially control functions to be exercised in accordance with social objectives and the principles of social economics. They may be classified as follows:

1. Obtaining a desirable relative volume of the various resources and a desirable division of labor between socio-economic units.

2. Securing a common denominator of comparison for measuring the relative importance of goods and the relative effectiveness of resource units through the use of money.

3. Determining the relative importance of goods and the relative effectiveness of resource units in producing them in a manner that will achieve social effectiveness in production, distribution, and consumption through pricing.

[1] By function is meant a proper activity in the control over the volume and utilization of the various resources through the organized economic units.

Chapter VI

Relative Volumes of Resources

THE OUTPUT PER WORKER

WE have assumed that a democratic society will have as one of its primary objectives the production of a large physical output of goods as a basis for the well-being of all of its members. It is one of the principles of social economics, stated and explained in the preceding pages, that a large volume of natural and cultural resources relative to the number of workers is conducive to a large output per worker. While it may appear difficult, if not impossible, for man to influence the absolute volumes of the natural resources, nevertheless, through our cultural resources, such as scientific knowledge and machines, we have greatly extended the volumes actually available. If a social economy achieves a large output per worker, it will be mainly because (1) the natural resources are wisely used and conserved, (2) the population is not so dense that the natural resources are utilized far into the stage of diminishing returns to the workers, (3) scientific knowledge is advanced, and (4) resources are utilized with the most effective technology possible.

THE VOLUME OF NATURAL RESOURCES

One of the main functions in the control of the volume of natural resources that are to be available for utilization is to guide the use of them to prevent present waste, deterioration, and future inaccessibility. This is especially important in the exploitation of such minerals as coal and petroleum; the coal veins may be inadequately worked or oil pools tapped in such a manner as to diminish the volume of oil that can be obtained in the future. Another function is not only to prevent the depletion of natural resources but to build them up as well, Forests may be conserved and expanded to make a larger volume available as the needs for wood products increase. Soils may easily be "mined" and whole regions become impoverished because the fertility of the land disappears; the fertility may also be conserved and, if depleted, it may be restored. This function is essentially that of making provision for the needs of the oncoming generations and can be adequately performed only when a society has a sense of continuity and an appreciation of the nature of waste. Provision for the future is the only check on the extent to which a social economy may make its natural resources available for immediate utilization, except when the use of more of them would not add anything to the total output, the point of diminishing total returns having been reached.

HUMAN RESOURCES

A primary function in a social economy is the attainment of the optimum effectiveness of an optimum population. This is a function of considerable importance and complexity. The actual determination of a population policy and the selection of methods for carrying it out are an extremely difficult task of social engineering, for changes in the economic effectiveness of a population, either through improved technical knowledge or a greater development of latent human capacities, will result in a change in the combination of the human with the other resources that will give the largest output per worker. Either a larger or a smaller population will become desirable with improvement or lack of improvement in technology, with changes in social objectives, and with changes in the division of labor between groups.

However, even a reasonably exact measurement of the economic consequences of population increase or decrease is probably impossible. There has never been any generally accepted estimate of the optimum population for a particular social economy, though certain regions may be generally considered too densely and others too sparsely populated at particular times. A region may be considered "too dense" in view of a shift in the division of labor within the world economy which makes it impossible to maintain as high a level of material well-being as in the past. Great Britain appears to be an example of such overpopulation. Then, too, the population may increase in a period when material well-being was not a primary social objective and when it becomes more important it is difficult to attain. Perhaps this may be the situation in some of the oriental countries.

Another aspect of the population problem in a social economy is significant in the formulation of policies. While an increase in the population may cause but a slight increase in the physical output of goods, and thus decrease the average output per worker, that average may decrease only slightly. This fact suggests that the division of the products of economic activity may be of more importance, from the standpoint of social well-being, than the size of the population.

In some respects the volume of population, in the economic sense, is amenable to considerable control, in other respects it is not. The volume and effectiveness of workers in a social economy will be influenced by (1) the birth and death rates, (2) the immigration and emigration, (3) mental and physical capacities and skills resulting from the biological and social inheritance, (4) willingness to work, (5) age, hour, and intensity restrictions, and (6) location and mobility of workers.

A population policy cannot be based entirely on economic considerations because material well-being is never the only social objective, and it may be sacrificed to attain what are considered more important objectives. A control over the natural increase or decrease in the population through influencing the birth rate is particularly difficult because of the non-economic factors involved. The views of sociologists, theologians, and militarists on the practice of birth control are apt to differ. Material well-being may be considered of less importance than religious or military factors.

Whatever the cause, there has been a rapid decline in the birth rate in recent decades, especially in the western hemisphere. It is apparently the result of an almost ubiquitous ambition of families to attain the highest possible material level of living. Whether it will move up or down in the future cannot be predicted. Some socio-economic units have attempted to arrest the decline by a condemnation of birth control and by encouraging earlier marriages or large families. While the results of such policies cannot be ascertained, they have not arrested the decline of the birth rate and the tendency of populations to become stable or actually decrease. It seems very probable that the attitudes and conditions which influence marriages and the size of families are subject to frequent and profound but unpredictable change, and that consequently the extent to which the birth rate in a social economy can be subjected to deliberate social control is uncertain.

Death rates have been diminished greatly by scientific knowledge and its application. A deliberate increase in the number of deaths is not tolerated except through war. Only the most callous individuals in this generation favor keeping the death rate high as a method of eliminating the so-called "unfit." Our sympathies are too well developed to permit a ruthless struggle for existence among human beings, even though they have not been developed far enough to prevent much higher rates among some groups than among others in the same communities. Through the application of scientific knowledge the death rate has been so rapidly diminished that populations generally have increased despite a declining birth rate. We may anticipate that in the future all societies will at all times do what they can to keep the death rate low.

Through the control of immigration and emigration the volume of population may be immediately affected. However, unless the flow of population is continuous the consequences may be only temporary. Emigration will not permanently reduce the population unless the birth rate and death rates are about equal after the migration. Immigration will result in an increase in the population unless it brings about an increase in the death rate or a decrease in the birth rate sufficient to offset its influence. Both immigration and emigration policies are also likely to be very considerably influenced by non-economic factors. The desire to plant colonies in sparsely settled regions does not have a purely economic source. Nations seek power and glory as well as material goods. Immigration may be encouraged if the impact of two cultures is regarded as desirable; it may be restricted if the cultures are too widely variant.

Undoubtedly the economic capacity of the human resources can be improved somewhat through the practice of eugenics and through the sterilization of those who have mental and physical defects that are transmitted in biological inheritance. *It is the social inheritance, however, that may be so regulated as to very greatly improve the economic capacities of workers.* This function of providing individuals with the opportunity to acquire the skills and knowledge which will make them more effective in economic activity is extremely important, especially in a society using a machine technology, for there is no limit to the increase in the volume of available human effort by this means as long as any individual is less effective than he might be in economic activity.

The volume and effectiveness of economic activity is also dependent upon the willingness of workers to perform particular tasks rapidly and well, so another most important function is that of providing an environment in which work is done willingly and effectively. The construction of such an environment is, of course, a difficult task, impossible of perfection.

A number of considerations will be influential in determining the age at which individuals will work, the amount of time they will spend at it, and the intensity with which they will carry it on. If all work hard for long hours a large volume of goods may be produced but there will be little time in which to consume it, the future economic capacity of the young may be impaired, and the average length of life in the nation may be shortened. There must somehow be a balancing between economic activity and leisure that will bring results harmonious with the accepted social objectives.

Finally, there is the function of placing human resources where they can be most effectively combined with the non-movable resources and of shifting them from one employment to another with the utmost possible facility, as the requirements of the production process necessitates. There are certain facts about human resources that make the function of providing for their mobility very important in a society using machine technology. Changes in needs and in technology constantly make the shifting or repricing of resources necessary. The movement of human beings from one place to another is not physically difficult and may be carried on to whatever extent is desirable provided adequate assurance of employment is given. A more significant aspect is the fact that by training and retraining individuals to perform various tasks they may continuously be made more effective in economic activity, and they need not become obsolete or be idle at all. This suggests that the marginal-money-products of individuals in the whole range of employment may be approximately equalized if proper opportunities are offered each one to become skilled in the production of the goods for which there is the greatest need.

CULTURAL RESOURCES

Cultural resources are those elements of the environment which mankind has acquired through the ages and which aid in economic activity. Some of them like scientific knowledge and economic institutions are intangible, while others like machines, buildings, and railroads are material objects. Scientific knowledge and institutional organization are limiting factors in production only in the sense that both have definite characteristics at a particular time, but they can be improved upon. Those material objects, which are produced resources, are limiting factors in that they are scarce relative to the needs for the goods which they help to obtain. It is through scientific knowledge, however, that natural and human resources are made more productive and the need for the accumulation of a larger volume of produced resources arises.

While all those institutions or social arrangements which aid in solving the basic economic problems are cultural resources, our immediate concern is with the functions involved in expanding scientific knowledge and in accumulating material objects as aids in future production.

THE EXTENSION AND UTILIZATION OF SCIENTIFIC KNOWLEDGE

Whether or not the population of a social economy grows, a continual improvement in the effectiveness of human effort will be necessary to obtain a larger and larger output of goods per worker. New and better consumers' goods, as well as more of them, are, we have assumed, socially desirable. This involves the use of resources in continuous scientific research and the application of new knowledge and inventions to the arts of production.

New processes and new machines frequently necessitate very great changes in the combination and utilization of resources in production units and industries, resulting in the scrapping of some resources and the shifting of others to different uses. While improvement in the effectiveness of economic activity is always to be welcomed, the manner and rate of change are very important for the human and resource costs may be so great as to overbalance the social gains unless the whole procedure is properly managed. Man-made resources may be built to last but a short time, with the expectation of early obsolescence; if they do become obsolete, their continued use or destruction will depend upon the probable effect on the present and future total volume of goods that will be made available for consumption. As long as their use will add to the total output of goods they are usable resources. Furthermore, displacement of hand workers by machines, as in the case of the hand weavers by power looms, will be accompanied by tremendous human cost, and goods cost as well, unless the workers are retrained and provided with new employment.

An improvement in technology must be widely adopted if the output of goods resulting from human effort is to be maximized. This means that improvements in processes and methods should be adopted by all production units as rapidly as possible and it suggests the desirability of making all scientific knowledge, techniques, and inventions a part of the social heritage throughout the world economy. For these reasons the creation of conditions favorable to the expansion of scientific knowledge and the invention of new processes and techniques is a highly important function. Once the inventions and discoveries are made, their utilization may be subjected to careful social control.

However, we must not count too heavily upon any particular rate of discovery in the sciences being maintained in the decades to come. According to one social scientist "material invention and discovery are unpredictable mutations in human culture" although "they can be encouraged by social effort."[1] We may

[1] Folsom, *op. cit.*, p. 502.

have "invented invention" but the consequences of our future efforts are uncertain.

PRODUCED MATERIAL RESOURCES—SOCIAL CAPITAL

The material objects produced and accumulated in the evolution of culture may be called social capital. They are made both possible and necessary by the advancement of science. To create them in the form of railroads, canals, power houses, buildings, or other such aids in production, necessitates the use of human and other resources. In building them a social economy diminishes the possible output of goods for direct consumption and produces objects which will make human effort more effective, and hence social well-being greater in the future. When social economy has natural and cultural resource volumes that are large relative to the number of workers, the per capita output may be so high that social well-being is not greatly diminished by the diversion of a considerable volume of resources into the production of more social capital. However, if the per capita output of goods is already low, or if certain groups in a social economy are made to consume less in order to produce more aids to production, social well-being may be seriously affected. One function in controlling their accumulation appears to be that of minimizing the decrease in social well-being that would occur from a lower per capita output of goods for immediate consumption. The creation of social capital may not require the actual reduction of the output of consumption goods, but merely a reduction in the volume that might have been produced. It appears that for many decades the advance of scientific knowledge has been so great that the flows of both goods and produced resources have constantly increased in volume.

Except for this balancing of the social desirability of present and future goods there is no limit to the volume of man-made resources that can be utilized up to the point where more of them would not add anything to the physical output of a social economy, the point of total diminishing returns to them; that would be the case if so many machines were produced that there were not enough workers to use them.

There is an almost complete mobility of potential produced

resources since the production of all possible kinds may be directed. An essential function in economic activity is to cause the production of those resources which will have the greatest money-products and hence, presumably, will make the greatest contribution to social well-being.

Communities, regions, or nations may also borrow goods and social capital from one another. The socio-economic unit which lends will have either fewer goods to consume or fewer resources to utilize for a time, and the borrowing unit will presumably have more resources for its workers to use and a higher per capita output. Such lending and borrowing would obviously increase the per capita output of the world economy though it might seriously restrict the per capita consumption of goods in the lending unit. The export of goods and social capital by Great Britain in the last century appears to have kept the level of material well-being much lower than it might have been for certain groups of the population at least. Even more tragic was the permanent loss of the exported goods and social capital through the exchange of claims on them or their equivalent for war materials during the Great War.

THE DIVISION OF LABOR BETWEEN SOCIO-ECONOMIC UNITS

Specialization between human groups is a consequence of the relative volumes and characteristics of the resources in each. Since both the human and cultural resources are subject to change over a period of time, the extent to which a social economy permits itself to specialize is a very serious problem. It is especially serious when the population grows as a result of a technological advantage which later disappears, for then the per capita output will be diminished as the degree of specialization declines. Technological advance made Great Britain the first powered-machine nation, but her advantage was temporary and now she is faced with less international specialization in the goods she produces and consequently a smaller per capita output of goods available for consumption. It seems quite possible that the population has grown too large considering the probable comparative advantage which the nation will have in the future.

Another aspect of group division of labor is that it is necessarily accompanied by group interdependence which may bring disastrous results unless there is a thorough and uninterrupted coördination throughout the whole productive process. The breakdown in the economic organization of the industrialized regions, beginning in 1929, is ample evidence of the lack of such coördination and it has caused considerable agitation in favor of group self-containment and of better methods of coördinating all economic activity.

Chapter VII

A Common Denominator of Comparison: Money

THE USES FOR MONEY

MONEY has two distinct but inseparable uses. It is a measuring device used to compare the relative importance of goods, and the relative effectiveness of resource units; it serves as a common denominator for comparison and combination. It is also used to facilitate the transfer of resources to production units and of goods to consumers. In a social economy that uses machine technology few individuals or groups produce the goods each needs; production units are separate entities in the economic process, each keeping an account of the resources utilized and of the contribution to the production of goods. Consequently there is a flow of resources to production units and of goods to consumers. In this process an interchange or transfer of resources and goods between individuals, groups, and production units is inevitable. Units of money serve as a medium of transfer in that they are recognized claims on goods and resources. Money may be defined as "any circulating medium generally recognized in economic intercourse as a means by which purchasing power is exercised. . . . Its possessor may offer it in exchange for any commodity or any service comprised in the communities aggregate supply of commodities and services."[1] It may be said that "whatever can serve and does serve as money, is money."[2]

A SATISFACTORY MONEY SYSTEM

The set of social arrangements which provide for a money unit as a measuring device and money units in some form to facilitate the transfer of goods and resources may be designated a *money system*. A satisfactory money system, one that would

[1] Hans Gluckstadt, *Theory of the Credit Standard*, p. 9. (P. S. King and Son, Ltd., 1932, London).
[2] *Ibid.*, p. 136.

perform its essential functions, will have certain characteristics. As a measuring unit and medium for transfer:

It will be so adaptable to changing conditions that it will reflect through prices the relative importance of goods and the relative effectiveness of resources but will not, in itself, be a cause of changes in prices generally; that is, it will not cause a general repricing of resources and goods.

As a medium for transfer:

It will be convenient in form; it will be sufficiently acceptable or recognized as a claim on goods and resources; it will have the lowest possible resource cost.

POSSIBLE FORMS OF MONEY

Money may take one or more of three forms:

1. A widely accepted commodity, such as cattle, wheat, tobacco, copper, gold, or silver.

2. A fiat or token, such as engraved paper or coins issued by the recognized sovereign power in the social economy and able to obtain resources and goods to exchange for the money units issued.

3. Other recognized claims, such as written orders on "funds" created by directly or indirectly basing them on resources or goods. Such funds are merely book accounts and may be increased or decreased as the need to facilitate transfers arises. The "written orders" cancel each other because all transfers are essentially goods or resources for goods or resources.

AS A MEASURING DEVICE

Prices are the reflections of the relative importance of goods and the relative effectiveness of resources in terms of money units. It is in this role of common denominator for comparison and combination that money should be a passive agent. The dollar, as a money unit, is a result of social arrangements. This is true in a very special sense for in itself a dollar in a society using a machine technology can be nothing but a recognized claim on goods or resources. It does not *determine* the relative importance of goods or the effectiveness of resources; it *measures* only in each case. The relative importance of goods depends upon who is able to obtain claims on them and upon the social objectives of a particular generation; the relative effectiveness of resources depends upon the types of goods considered most important and upon the relative volume of the resources available for use in producing them. In other words, the goods are evaluated in terms of other goods and the resources in terms of their usefulness in producing goods. The organization of resource utilization in an effective manner will depend upon the ease with which these various comparisons can be made; a satisfactory money system will permit them to be made without interfering with the smoothness of the flow of resources into production and of goods into consumption.

A distinction should be carefully made between the volume of claims or purchasing power over the outputs of production units and the volume of transfers made in the process of producing and consuming the goods; and also between the volume of transfers over a period of time and the volume of money units in existence at a particular moment. The volume of claims is a consequence of the volume of output while the volume of money units used is a consequence of the volume of exchanges or transfers. The same goods or resources may be transferred many times and the same money used many times, but the same goods may be consumed only once. Diagram C may serve to illustrate this point:

Diagram C
Actual Claims and the Volume of Transfers

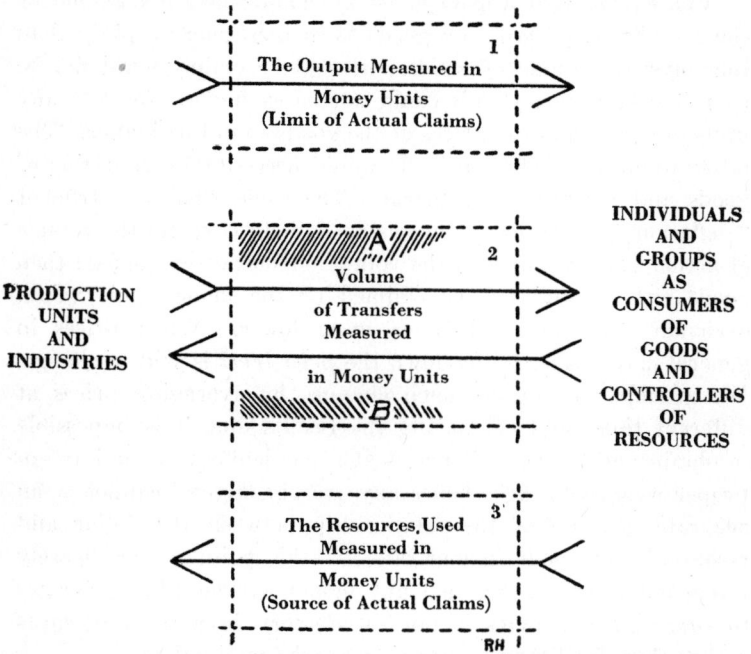

1 The Output Measured in Money Units (Limit of Actual Claims)

PRODUCTION UNITS AND INDUSTRIES

2 Volume of Transfers Measured in Money Units

(shaded area A, shaded area B)

INDIVIDUALS AND GROUPS AS CONSUMERS OF GOODS AND CONTROLLERS OF RESOURCES

3 The Resources Used Measured in Money Units (Source of Actual Claims)

RH

NOTE: These rectangles are drawn to indicate contraction and expansion as conditions change. There is no necessary percentage relationship between Rectangle 2 and the others. Rectangle 2 represents the volume of transfers required in the flow of resources to production units and of the goods produced to consumers. The shaded area "A" in it represents the transfers that are made from production units to individuals in groups without the use of money; a farm, as a production unit, supplies food for the family which cultivates it. No particular percentage relationship between such transfers and the total volume is implied. The shaded area "B" represents the total number of money units in existence at a particular moment but no particular percentage relationship to the total volume of transfers is implied.

The outstanding fact illustrated in this diagram is that the basic exchange is resources for goods. The necessity for pricing resources in order to obtain the most effective apportionment and combination of them and for pricing goods to compare their relative importance and money cost we have dealt with at length. The total volumes of resources utilized and of goods in terms of money must be equal if the economic process is to operate smoothly, but the total volume of money used and the total volume of money transfers are dependent upon the social arrangements for controlling and utilizing resources and for dividing up and using the claims on outputs.

Consequently, if a money system should make it possible for the actual money claims on goods to increase more rapidly than the physical volume of goods, either some claims could not be exercised or a money unit could not be exchanged for as many units of goods, and the prices of the goods would be higher. The latter would be "inflation." It would necessitate a repricing of goods and resources in general. The same would be true of "deflation" where the money system failed to expand the volume of actual money claims as the volume of output expanded; then goods either could not be claimed or the money unit would exchange for more, prices becoming lower. When prices in general move either up or down the *price level* is said to change. We attempt to measure such changes by averaging prices at different times and comparing the results, but it is impossible to obtain and average all prices at a particular time and assign proper weights to each; hence any average secured cannot be an accurate measure of the relationship between the dollar and resources and goods in general. At this point we are merely interested in suggesting that any money system which operates to *cause* such changes is not satisfactory because it disrupts rather than facilitates comparisons and combinations.

However, the money system is not the only possible cause of price level changes and even though it were quite flexible it would not be able to prevent the repricing of vast groups of goods and resources. It would be possible, for example, for the prices of most goods and resources to be lowered while only the prices of human resources would remain unchanged or be raised—as a result of technological progress. Continuous and widespread repricing of goods and resources is quite desirable as long as it tends to promote a socially more effective utilization of resources. But if repricing is caused by the inflexibility of the money system it may diminish rather than increase social effectiveness in the use of resources by making comparisons less accurate and thus disrupting the economic process.

AS A MEDIUM FOR TRANSFERS

As a tangible claim on goods and resources money becomes a medium for exchange or transfer. If its form is such that it can be easily carried or transported without danger of loss, and if it can be transfered in any number of units, the requirements for convenience in form would be met. If it were freely used in exchange for goods and resources in an economy, in no way preventing the smooth flow of resources into production and goods into consumption, it would meet the requirements for acceptibility. Lastly if a minimum of resources are required in obtaining a sufficient number of money units as a tool for facilitating transfers, a satisfactory money would be obtained at the lowest possible resource cost.

COMMODITY MONEY

Now the only form of money which could not conceivably be satisfactory as a measuring device or as a medium for transfers in a society using a machine technology is a commodity money, such as a definite unit of cattle, tobacco, silver, or gold. A commodity, used as a medium of exchange either directly or indirectly as well as a measuring unit, would constitute the volume of claims on the output. Consequently, unless there was a change in the volume of the commodity money or in the number of times each unit were used, every time there was a change in the physical volume of output, there would arise the necessity of repricing resources and goods simply because the volume of money units was not flexible. There is no reason to believe that the volume of a commodity or its velocity (number of times used in a given period) would change as the need for money changes. This means that a commodity such as gold must inevitably be unsatisfactory both as a measuring unit and as medium of exchange.

THE GOLD STANDARD

If gold were used as a measuring unit with a fixed number of grains designated as the dollar and with the other types of money made interchangeable with it, the result would be a gold standard. Gold coins would be struck out of all gold brought to the mints for that purpose. The alleged advantages of a gold dollar are that, being a commodity that is lasting, divisible, malleable, and not subject to much fluctuation in the total volume in existence, it would provide a *sound* and *stable* measuring unit. That a gold dollar has these advantages is wholly illusory.

Any money that is recognized as a claim on goods or resources would appear to be sound for all practical purposes. Where a gold standard is used and other forms of money made interchangeable there would always be grave danger that this interchangeability between gold and other forms of money would overshadow the exchangeability of money units for goods and resources. A situation might easily arise in which money units that were supposed to be exchangeable for gold could not be exchanged for it and the whole pricing system unnecessarily disrupted by interfering with the exchangeability between money units and goods and resources which is essential to a satisfactory money system.[3]

But, it is with respect to stability or its influence on the level of prices that the gold dollar fails miserably as a measuring unit. If gold, as a commodity, were to have any real influence on the level of prices it would make for great fluctuation because there could not be any automatically adjusted relationship between the physical volume of gold and the need for it as money or as a basis for other forms of money. The price level would constantly have to be adjusted to the volume of gold in order to obtain sufficient money units to carry on the necessary transfers. The volume of money claims on the output of production must be based upon that output and not upon the amount of gold existing anywhere. It appears reasonable to hold that a gold dollar, if actually used in exchange would constantly upset the price level. On the other hand if gold were made interchangeable with other forms of money and a reserve set up to

[3] The closing of all banks in the United States in March, 1933, and the subsequent impounding of the stock of gold by the United States Treasury is a classic example of this state of affairs. However, the banks not only could not pay out gold, they could not get other forms of money because the resources and goods upon which the banks' assets were based through the promissory notes of the customers were no longer available at the assumed prices to meet the claims of the bank and its depositors. The system of transferring goods and resources for goods and resources through the use of money broke down also.

guarantee redemption it would be conceivable that at certain times the volume of claims on goods might be checked because of the smallness of the quantity of gold held as reserve against the other forms of money used, regardless of the actual volume of goods to be transferred, thus forcing goods and resources to exchange at lower prices. At other times the volume of claims might be expanded as a result of new discoveries of gold or new methods of reducing gold ores, thus causing the same volume of goods and resources to be repriced on a higher level. Such possibilities force the conclusion that commodities such as gold have no merit whatever as money.

As a matter of fact, even though the gold standard has been in use for some decades, there is no acceptable evidence that either the volume of money used in exchange or the volume of claims on the output and hence the purchasing power of the dollar, has had any definite relationship at all with the volume of gold dollars. During this same period the development of machine technology has made vastly greater specialization and vastly larger outputs of goods possible. While the volume of gold has fluctuated there has been no correlation with the need for money. Other forms of money have been easily provided making it appear that there is not the slightest need for even a metallic base for the money system. As a unit of measurement the gold dollar has been and must inevitably be a fiction; the grains of gold in a dollar may be stabilized but that is a fact of little economic significance. As other forms of money have come into wide use the money system has in reality become "managed" because their volumes are subject to deliberate control, and if the system has not properly performed its functions it is a result of uncoördinated or bad management.

Furthermore, a commodity is not satisfactory for use in an international money system. The advantages of gold, as an international commodity money, for example, are alleged to be the stability it gives to the exchange relationships between the various national money units and the automic balancing of payments between countries through the importation and exportation of gold as a universally acceptable commodity. It is supposed that this would provide an international common denominator for pricing. Again the advantages of gold or any commodity money appear to be wholly illusory.

As long as the exchange of resources and goods between countries balance, their money units will remain in fixed relationships, but when they get out of balance a shift of gold from one country to another is supposed to result in a balancing of payments through causing the prices to rise in the country with the excessive exports and to fall in the one with the excessive imports. Higher prices would supposedly cause a country to export less and import more, while lower prices would have the opposite effect. It does not appear desirable to maintain a fixed or stable relationship between the money units of the different nations if it has to be done by gold shipments, assuming they would be really effective in changing price levels. Such price level changes would upset the economic processes and unless foreign trade is an extremely dominant factor in the economic life of a social economy the interference of gold movements on the domestic price level would be too great an inconvenience to warrant a fixed exchange relationship between its money unit and those of other countries. It would be far simpler and less disastrous to the economic processes to permit the exchange relationships between national money units to fluctuate until volume of imports and exports were always equal in terms of those money units. There is no acceptable proof that the various countries have permitted or would permit gold shipments to influence their respective price levels. If they did not, the use of gold would not last long as a means of balancing payments. And, indeed, it has not.

Perhaps the use of gold as an international money has been bound up with the nonsensical notion that a nation should attempt to maintain a "favorable balance of trade," that is, always export so many goods (including services) and resources that the import of some gold will be necessary. Just how it would be possible to maintain such a balance of trade and also use gold as international money has never been explained. In any case the interference of gold shipments with domestic price levels would be both unnecessary and undesirable; it would merely delay an inevitable balancing of imports and exports in terms of money.

It is immediately obvious that the use of gold or any commodity money as a "circulating medium" is impossible and undesirable when the volume of transfers is very great. Gold coins, for example, would be too small for use in many exchanges and too cumbersome in others. There would be a great loss from wear. Finally, gold has a high resource cost compared with other possible forms of money. Despite the widespread use of a gold standard in recent decades, gold has been abandoned as a circulating medium. It seems wise to eliminate it from the money system entirely.

FIAT AND TOKEN MONEY

This is a form of money created by the state, the sovereign power of a social economy. As paper or coin it has a low resource cost, is easily adjusted in volume to meet the needs for facilitating certain types of transfers and hence makes a satisfactory element in the money system. Its volume should not, of course, be changed in such degree as would cause a repricing of goods and resources. It is a recognized medium for transfers ultimately, perhaps, because the state can obtain, through taxation or otherwise, the resources and goods with which to substantiate it as a claim on them. For a large volume of transfers, however, this form is not the most convenient or most adaptable money. Its use is limited to those individuals who wish to carry with them and use a form of money that is a recognized claim on resources and goods throughout a social economy. Consequently it is confined to the relatively small transfers and is a supplement to a more satisfactory form of money.

WRITTEN ORDERS ON FUNDS

The creation of funds upon which written orders for transfer may be made provides the most satisfactory form of money in a social economy which uses a machine technology and hence must provide for a large volume of transfers, some of which must involve large amounts of resources and goods. These funds represent actual goods or resources, directly or indirectly; they are merely book accounts. The written orders on them may be created for use as money in whatever volume is necessary to facilitate transfers. Such written orders have small resource-cost and are very convenient because they can be made out for whatever amount is desired. They cancel each other as funds are constantly being drawn upon and added to. The best example of this form of money is, of course, the present day bank checks drawn upon the funds as deposits in the banks. The deposits are in large measure based upon the so-called loans and discounts which are in turn based upon actual goods and resources. Within a country and between countries these written orders are given in exchange and when collected, cancel each other as between nations, regions, communities, and persons. The result is the transfer with great ease and rapidity of the goods and resources in whatever volume is necessary.

The question that inevitably arises when it is suggested that this is the form of money which most nearly meets the requirements in a satisfactory money system is—what is the dollar? The answer is that the dollar is the volume of resources and goods for which it will exchange; its purchasing power is and must inevitably be a result of the pricing system.

Chapter VIII
The Pricing Process

THE PURPOSES OF PRICING

GOODS and resources are priced in order that social effectiveness in production, distribution, and consumption may be maximized. As we have repeated many times, there must be some method devised for determining the types and quantities of goods that shall be produced, how they shall be produced, and who shall consume them; the relative importance of goods and their relative resource-costs must somehow be measured. Prices serve as a basis for comparison however, since they are themselves the result of social arrangements, the success of the pricing process in promoting social well-being will depend upon the nature of these arrangements. Prices merely reflect the objectives and attitudes that dominate an economic order, and they cannot be separated from the whole social process in which we attempt to attain what is considered worth while in the manner that is accepted as appropriate. It is obvious that prices and the pricing process are extremely important in their possible influence on resource utilization; they have an importance that transcends the field of economic comparison. One social philosopher makes this point as follows:

> The price of a thing, we say, is a material matter which has nothing to do with its higher values, and never can have. This, however, is bad philosophy, in economics as in religion. The pecuniary values are members of the same general system as the moral and aesthetic values, and it is part of their function to put the latter upon the market. To separate them is to cripple both, and to cripple life itself by cutting off the healthy interchange among its members. Our line of progress lies, in part at least, not over commercialism but through it; the dollar is to be reformed rather than suppressed. Our system of production and exchange is a very great achievement, not more on the mechanical side than in the social possibilities latent in it. Our next task seems to be to fulfill these possibilities, to enlarge and humanize the system by bringing it under the guidance of a comprehensive social and ethical policy.[1]

[1] Charles Horton Cooley, *Social Process*, pp. 327-28.

In a social economy in which individuals and groups are permitted to obtain claims on goods in general, it will be possible for them to choose between various types and volumes of goods for consumption. Where there is such liberty of choice in consumption it becomes necessary to determine the prices at which various outputs will be taken by consumers and the money-costs of those outputs to the production units. The purpose is, of course, to hit upon a price at which the output of an industry is the same as the amount taken by consumers. In the pricing of resources the purpose is to reflect their marginal-money-products in all uses and enable a least-cost combination in production units. Resource pricing will inevitably have considerable influence upon the division of the claims on the products of economic activity. The pricing of goods and resources will, therefore, determine the extent to which resource utilization will actually promote social well-being.

THE PRICING PROCESS

Two possible procedures for pricing goods and resources are apparent. A procedure may be established under which individuals, groups, or production units which wish to exchange money for certain goods or services can make offers constituting a *demand,* while individuals, groups, or production units which control goods and resources and wish to exchange them for money can also make offers, constituting the *supply.* The result would be a *market* which may be described as follows:

A market in economic parlance is the area within which the forces of demand and supply converge to establish a single price. It may be viewed geographically as a physical extent of territory, or it may be viewed as a more or less organized group of individuals whose bids and offers disclose the supply and demand situation and thereby establish the price.[2]

The other procedure is to fix prices for goods and resources through some sort of *authority* within the social economy, leaving to individuals and groups the choice of various types and volumes of goods they will consume at the prices fixed and leaving to those in control of production units and industries the choice

[2] C. O. Hardy, in *Encyclopaedia of Social Science,* X, 131. (The Macmillan Company, 1933).

of types and quantities of the various resources to be combined and utilized in each. There is not really so much difference in the two procedures as may at first appear, for both are the consequences of social arrangements and would produce similar results under similar circumstances.

PRICING THROUGH MARKETS

A market is only one of many social arrangements which aid in the solution of the basic economic problems. Indeed, a market is no really definite arrangement. There are innumerable conditions under which a market mechanism might function, and the prices which result from its operation will depend upon these conditions. The same market might bring forth many different prices for the same volume and type of goods if changes were made in the environment in which it operates.

Through market mechanisms extremely important decisions may be made, such as:

1. The kinds and quantities of consumption goods produced.
2. The relative volumes of social capital and consumption goods produced.
3. The prices that are to be paid for both consumption goods and resources.
4. The kinds and volumes of resources that will be available for use in production in so far as they can be increased and decreased.

Such matters are so important that the environment in which a market operates must be carefully created if it is to function so as to bring about social effectiveness in resource utilization. As man-made arrangements, markets are very much amenable to selfish individual and group manipulation. The forces behind market situations and the market practices themselves are so interwoven in the whole environment as to make deliberate social control inevitable. For example, the kind and quantity of consumption goods which can be sold in a given market will depend upon the division of purchasing power, which in turn is a result of the social arrangements that determine the quantity, quality and control of resources.

The use of markets as measurement devices may be controlled or limited in two ways:

1. Certain measurements of the importance of goods may be taken away from the markets completely. This has been done in considerable degree with respect to the provision for education.
2. The environment in which the market operates may be controlled by:
   a. Regulating the conditions of demand and supply; and
   b. Controlling the rules or procedures under which market measurements are determined.

To illustrate this point, in the market for human resources (1) child or other labor may be prohibited and taken out of the market entirely, or the wages, hours and working conditions may be fixed through public authority; (2) the volume of human resources may be influenced through control over the birth and death rates or over immigration and emigration; (3) an environment in which individuals would have approximately equal opportunity to carry on the various types of economic activity may be created; (4) the bargaining power of those buying and selling labor may be equalized through collective bargaining arrangements.

There is surely nothing sacred or immutable about markets as institutional arrangements. Their function is to provide a method of determining the prices of resources and goods in so far as such a method will contribute to social effectiveness in production, in distribution, and in consumption. The environment in which they operate must be carefully controlled if these objectives are to be attained.

PRICING BY AUTHORITY

Pricing through authorities, constituted as price-fixing boards, commissions or agencies, is only a more direct procedure than the use of markets. A price-fixing authority would have to determine, through experience and fact-finding, the situation with respect to the probable volume of goods that would be consumed at various prices and the money-costs of various volumes of output. In pricing resources the marginal money-product of a particular resource group would be estimated. Prices would have to be constantly readjusted to meet changing conditions in an effort to keep the flow of resources into production and goods into consumption at a maximum. Of course the prices would also be fixed so as to harmonize with the accepted social objectives; but the possible range of price variation would be very small, and the only really effective way to improve unsatisfactory conditions in production, consumption and distribution would be through a change in the general environment which makes certain prices more or less inevitable.

Chapter IX

Pricing Goods for Consumption

PRICING POLICIES

WHETHER prices are fixed directly by constituted authority or indirectly through markets, various changes in the dynamic factors of resource utilization will require definite pricing policies. We will now inquire into the problems of pricing under the following conditions respectively:

1. When the flow of a good from production into consumption is "in balance."
2. When consumers will no longer take the output of an industry at a price equal to the least-money-cost combination.
3. When consumers will take more than the output of an industry at a price equal to the least-money-cost combination.
4. When technological improvement lowers the least-money-cost.
5. When the money cost of some of the resources used in an industry increases.

In analyzing these problems the usual assumption, that the proper price policy is the one which will maximize the results of human effort in economic activity, is made.

THE IDEAL OUTPUT OF AN INDUSTRY

When the production units of an industry have achieved the lowset possible least-money-cost combination and when the number of production units is such that their combined output is just the volume which consumers will take at a price equal to the money cost, then an industry has the ideal and output resource combination. The flow of production and the flow of consumption of the good is in balance. The proper price would obviously be the one which will not upset this balance as long as other conditions permit it to last.

WHEN THE OUTPUT OF AN INDUSTRY IS TOO LARGE

As the needs of individuals and groups change, the output of some industries can no longer be sold at a price equal to the money cost, even when the production units are operating at the least money-cost combination. What price policy should a social economy encourage through the pricing mechanism? From the point of view of social effectiveness in production, resources should not be left idle, so those which are committed to a particular use should be repriced, the prices being lowered until the output of the industry is being produced at a money cost at which it will be taken by consumers. Then, as these non-shiftable resources, such as machines, wear out they would not be replaced unless the probable money-product would equal the money cost of new ones, and the shiftable resources would be transferred to other industries. In this way the number of production units in the industry would be diminished until there was a balance between production and consumption again, at whatever least-cost combination was obtained when the resources were correctly apportioned between uses. Price changes should obviously be made as rapidly as the physical readjustment of resources between industries takes place, the basic objective always being that of full utilization of the resources regardless of how low it becomes necessary to price them.

WHEN THE OUTPUT OF AN INDUSTRY IS TOO SMALL

When consumers, either individual or collective, will take a larger volume of goods at a price equal to the least-cost than is being produced by an industry, two alternative price and production policies appear possible.

1. The output can be increased beyond the least-cost combination and prices fixed according to the additional cost of the last unit which will be claimed by consumers at the increased price.

2. Production units can continue to operate at their least-cost combination while more production units are organized. Prices would remain unchanged and, if the stock of the particular good was depleted some consumers would have to wait until the output was increased.

Which of these policies is followed will depend upon the institutional "set up" of the particular social economy. Perhaps each would serve equally well to indicate the desirability of shifting more resources to the industry, thus creating more or larger production units. There are, however, some considerations which suggest the superiority of one policy over the other under certain conditions.

The first policy will enable a more immediate increase in output through adding variable resource units past the least-cost combination. This would result in a *surplus* over total-money-cost and would give rise to the problem of determining what to do with it, but it would be strong evidence of the necessity for a reapportionment of resources. The surplus arises because the price would be fixed in line with the cost of the additional units of output and it would be greater than the average cost. Both the output and the price would rise until consumers would merely just claim the output at a price equal to the cost of the last unit or units added. We may use the fruit canning illustration to show the consequences of this policy:

TABLE X

TOTAL MONEY INCOME AND TOTAL MONEY COST

No. of Workers	Output Per Day	Total Money Cost Machine Line $200 Workers $4	Average Money Cost per 100 Cans	Average Additional Money Cost Per 100 Cans	Total Money Income at $30 Per 100 Cans	Above or Below Total Cost
10	0.5	$240	$480.00	$80.00	$ 15.00	—225.00
20	3.0	280	93.33	16.00	90.00	—190.00
30	6.4	320	50.01	11.76	192.00	—128.00
40	10.0	360	36.00	11.11	300.00	— 60.00
50	13.6	400	29.40	11.11	408.00	+ 8.00
60	16.9	440	26.04	12.12	507.00	+ 67.00
70	19.6	480	24.48	14.82	588.00	+108.00
80	21.7	520	23.97	19.05	651.00	+131.00
90	23.0	560	24.35	30.77	690.00	+130.00
100	23.7	600	25.32	57.14	711.00	+111.00
110	23.7	640	27.00	....	711.00	+ 71.00
120	23.4	680	29.05	....	702.00	+ 22.00

According to this illustration the output would be around 2,300 cans per day because the average cost of the additional output resulting from increasing the number of workers from 80 to 90 is $30.76. However, the average total cost is under $24.35 at that combination and there will be a surplus over total cost of $131.00. When the output is increased until the marginal-cost equals the price to consumers the surplus over total cost will be maximized. It must be emphasized that this surplus is an evidence of a malapportionment of resources and social effectiveness in production requires its elimination through a reapportionment of resources as soon as that is physically possible.

This price policy has the merit of permitting those consumers who have the relatively greatest preference for the good to obtain it by eliminating others through raising the price. If the claims on goods are divided in a socially effective manner, those with the greatest preference might well be given the opportunity to consume the good since their "need" for it is relatively most pressing. However, in case the good, which is for a time limited in quantity, was essential to the well-being of all individuals it would be necessary to prorate it to consumers, thus limiting their range of choice with respect to the quantity that could be obtained.

On the other hand, if the claims on goods are not divided in a socially effective manner, higher prices may squeeze out those with small incomes and social well-being would be diminished rather than increased by such a procedure.

The second price and production policy would appear sensible if there was a stock of the goods awaiting consumption and it would be possible to increase the flow of production before that stock was entirely depleted. A flow into consumption larger than the flow of output would indicate the desirability of shifting more resources into the production of the particular good. The stock awaiting consumption would be a sort of buffer, making price changes unnecessary and enabling all who wish to consume at the existing price to do so. This procedure would not be contrary to the principle of using the marginal-money-product of groups of resource units to indicate their correct apportionment between employments. It is merely a method of anticipating the necessity for reapportionment and of carrying it out without necessarily changing the prices of either goods or resources. An equalization of the marginal-money-product of a particular group of resource units in all employments would still remain a basic requirement for their correct apportionment.

This same policy might well be followed even when there was no stock awaiting consumption if the necessary adjustment in the number or size of production units to produce a larger output at the least-cost combination could be made quickly and consumers would not have to wait long for a sufficient output to fill their needs. The policy of waiting for future outputs might also be followed regardless of the relative degree of preferences if the social well-being would not be greatly affected, that is, if the unfilled needs were not especially important anyway.

WHEN TECHNOLOGICAL IMPROVEMENT CHANGES THE LEAST-MONEY-COST COMBINATION

With technological improvement a new and lower least-money-cost combination becomes possible. What price policies shall be followed in bringing about a readjustment of the size and number of production units? Should the new least-cost be discovered and adopted as a price for the good, necessitating a repricing of the non-shiftable resources and causing the stock of goods awaiting consumption to be completely depleted? Or should the new and lower price be put into effect only after the improvement has spread throughout the industry and the reorganization of production units taken place, thus permitting some production units to obtain prices above their least-money-cost? Again we may say that whichever policy is followed will depend upon the social arrangements, and it may be a matter of little ultimate social consequence. The important matter is the spread of the improvement throughout the industry as rapidly as possible and the readjustment of resource units between industries, bringing the prices of the goods down to the new low money cost when the necessary adjustments have been made, if not before.

WHEN THE MONEY COST OF SOME RESOURCES INCREASES FOR A PRODUCTION UNIT

It may be that an increased need for some of the goods which a particular group of resource units helps to produce will cause an increase in the marginal money product of that group. A production unit producing a certain good, the need for which has not changed, will then be faced with higher money cost for resource units of that type. How will the least money cost combination be affected? That will depend upon the nature of the other resource units used by the production unit. In the fruit canning plant illustration, if the cans should increase in price, due to the increased cost of larger volumes of tin plate, the least-money-cost combination would be affected. In case the other resources were shiftable to different employments a readjustment of money cost and output would occur, probably lowering the latter and increasing the former, of canned fruit. However, if any of the resources, such as the machine-line, could not be shifted, it would be necessary to reprice them in order to keep them in continuous use. Such repricing might result in both the least-money-cost combination and the price of canned fruit remaining unchanged until the non-shiftable resources were worn out and not replaced.

THE PRACTICAL PROBLEM OF PRICING A GOOD

So far in our analysis we have avoided the practical matter of the physical possibility of finding and maintaining the ideal least-money-cost combination in each and every production unit. Actually only a rough approximation is possible, but that does not make its attainment any less desirable from the point of view of social effectiveness in the use of resources.

A number of factors will operate to cause variation in the actual or apparent money-costs of production units. They are:

1. Natural forces and unavoidable accidents;
2. Physical limitations in shifting some of the resource units;
3. The failure to reprice some of the resource units;
4. Variation in the effectiveness of human effort at different times and under different psychological circumstances.

Perhaps the most unstable production conditions exist in agriculture where climatic conditions and insect pests are so variable in their influence upon the outputs of production units. Not only will such conditions cause variation between production units during the same year but for the same production units in different years. Furthermore, accidents injuring machines or workers will increase the money cost of some production units over that of others.

Groups of workers, apparently similar in effectiveness, will vary in their actual outputs at different times. Changes in the psychological mood of the workers in a plant, a community or a nation may cause considerable variation in output. Such variations may be controlled where they are understood, but we have little hope of being able to account fully for all of them.

Even though better techniques, processes, or machines become known it takes time to actually become acquainted with their possibilities throughout an industry and to adopt them to use. It would, furthermore, be a difficult matter to reprice accurately all the resource units committed to particular uses in order that they might harmonize with the results of new inventions. Where the necessary repricing could be carried out but is not, the money cost has little significance; it cannot be used as a guide in apportioning resources or in pricing goods. But there might be circumstances under which accurate repricing would be difficult because the consequence of changes in needs or of new inventions would not be readily apparent.

As a consequence of these dynamic factors in an industry, the determination of a proper price policy is not a simple matter. Indeed there is no obviously "correct" price. If a price is fixed which is equal to the money-cost of the production units which have not been as effective as others, some of the production units will have total-money-revenues greater than their total-money-cost while others may have greater total-money-costs than total-money-revenues. The former may be said to have a money-surplus and the latter a money-deficit from operations. If the price were fixed near the lowest possible least-money-cost combination perhaps a large number of production units would have money deficits according to their bookkeeping systems. Again we must say that the price policy adopted is of little consequence if the production units in the industry shift resource combinations as rapidly as it is physically possible in order to attain the most effective combination, and if resources are ruthlessly repriced, especially the non-human, when marginal-money-products change. Under whatever price policy is followed, it will be necessary for the social economy to make some provision for the absorption of the deficits and surpluses into the process of dividing the claims on goods in general among the members of the society.

Variation between production units in the money cost of a good does not indicate an incorrect combination of resource units if it is due to natural, accidental, or human causes of the type just described. However, if a surplus or deficit occurs in a production unit as a result of changed needs of consumers or of improved technology it indicates the desirability of either repricing some resources or of shifting resource units between production units and industries.

Chapter X

The Pricing of Resources

A COMPLEX FUNCTION

THIS is a most intricate function in a social economy using a machine technology. It not only involves an interacting relationship between the prices of goods and the prices of resources but it is also a part of the mechanism through which the claims on the goods produced are kept in balance with the prices of the goods to be claimed. From the point of view of social effectiveness in production there appears to be one main objective in the pricing of resources; namely—*To keep them in constant use producing the most needed goods in the most effective combination.*

The price of a resource unit is supposed to reflect the marginal-money-product of the group of similar units, all of which have been correctly apportioned between possible uses. Such a price will depend upon the volume of purchasing power consumers are willing to use in obtaining the goods its particular type helps to produce, and also upon the relative available volume of the other resources with which it is combined. The price of an acre of land that will produce citrous fruit, for example, will depend upon its own volume relative to the need for its product, and upon the abundance of the human and other resources which utilize it. If its volume is small relative to the needs of consumers and if other resources are so abundant that they utilize it far into the stage of diminishing return to themselves, its imputed marginal-money-product and hence its price will be "high." Changes in either of these situations would necessitate repricing.

Since there are continuous changes in the nature and volume of needed goods, and since scientific knowledge makes other cultural and natural resources more and more available, thus constantly causing change in the correct physical combination of resources in the economic units, the prices of both goods and resources must constantly change. Out of the pricing process, however, must come a balancing between the money claims on goods arising from the pricing of resources and the money prices of the output as it flows from the production units, if production and consumption are to be balanced at the maximum physical output of the most needed goods.

THE COST OF RESOURCES AND THEIR PRICES

Neither the human nor the money cost of most resources in use at a particular time can have much, if any, influence on their respective prices. Of course, land and other natural resources have no cost, though they must be priced in order that they may be economized. Those processes, techniques, and scientific facts which are available for use everywhere need not be priced for they have become "free resources," a part of our social heritage; though they may have had a tremendous human cost, they need not be priced for they need not be economized. Human resources have both human and money cost but the pricing of them can never be influenced by such costs. No records of the money-cost of human resources could conceivably be kept, and they would not be a proper basis for pricing even if they were available. The prices of human resources might be a factor in influencing the size of families and the willingness to undergo training for particular tasks; in so far as that is the case there might be some connection between the number and skill of workers and the prices of labor-force. However, since individuals may work for many years, the dynamic factors behind the pricing process make it unlikely that the marginal-money-product of a particular type of human resource would have any close relationship with the money cost of acquiring a particular skill for any period of time. The only object of pricing human resources is to make it possible to economize them.

So it is also with the produced resources that must be economized; they must be constantly repriced as their marginal-money-products change, regardless of their money cost. It would seem, however, that there would necessarily have to be some relationship between the money cost of produced resources and their prices in the production process. Why should a machine-line for a canning plant be constructed if its money-product during its use would not equal its money cost? Such a relationship does, of course, exist at the time the resources are produced and to obtain such a relationship is a primary purpose of the pricing process, but if produced resources are durable and are used over a period of time, either technological progress or changes in the needs of consumers will necessitate repricing them.

With technological improvement there arises the necessity of deciding whether or not obsolete equipment or other resources should be immediately scrapped or utilized until worn out. The solution of this problem appears to depend upon the pricing process. It is as follows: other resources should utilize the obsolete equipment as long as their marginal-money-product is as great as in any other use, including the making and use of new equipment. The result would be a reduction in the money-product and hence, the price of the obsolete equipment to zero before it would be scrapped. One aspect of technological progress cannot be emphasized too strongly—as improvements are made they should take place without causing waste or idleness of resources, if scientific progress is to be reflected into the social well-being.

HUMAN RESOURCES SEEM TO REQUIRE SPECIAL TREATMENT IN PRICING

In any social economy there would be some relationship between the price of the labor of a worker and the claim he can make on the goods produced; his income as a worker would be a part of this total claim on goods. Now technological progress may replace workers and cause their labor to be priced lower, at least until it could be shifted to other uses. The work of others might be priced higher until more could be trained for the new tasks. Changes in the needs of consumers for certain goods would have similar results. But human resources, as we have already pointed out, are extremely shiftable where a social economy really makes provision for training and retraining workers for whatever tasks seem to require them. A reduction in the claims on goods of some workers would reduce their well-being and thus defeat the social objectives in resource utilization. Because of these apparent facts *it would seem sensible for a social economy to fix and keep stable, in terms of money-units, the prices on the various types of human effort in whatever manner would effectively accomplish the social objectives; and then cause the repricing of other resources and the goods produced to reflect the changes in needs and in technology.* The result of such a policy in pricing human resources would be a stability in the money claims on goods but a lowering of the prices of other resources and of the goods produced, as the effectiveness of human effort in production increased. This pricing policy would obviously necessitate elaborate social arrangements for shifting human resources by further training, if necessary, as rapidly and as extensively as conditions warranted, while keeping their money incomes constant. It would cause a decrease in the prices generally affected by technological progress and the money claims going to workers would exchange for more goods, though remaining constant in volume.

THE PRICING OF RESOURCES AND THE DIVISION OF THE OUTPUT FOR CONSUMPTION

We must now face the problem of the relationship between the pricing of resources and social effectiveness in the division of the output and its consumption. We have pointed out that the pricing of resource units was essential to economizing them in production. We have pointed out further that the source of claims on goods must be through claims on the output of resources.

Some aspects of this problem are obvious:

1. A democratic society which holds the well-being of every member of society of equal importance will require a fairly equal division of income (including collective consumption) in order to provide each individual with equal opportunity for the good life, whatever it is conceived to be. It has been pointed out before that one of the conditions under which the division of output will maximize social well-being is the production and consumption of those goods which are most needed from the social point of view.

2. The use of machine technology also requires a fairly equal division of claims on goods because full use of it can be made only through mass production. If there is mass production there must be mass consumption.

3. If each individual or family receives approximately the volume of claims on goods (income) considered essential to the good life, the claims arising from the pricing of human effort would have to be supplemented by claims arising from the pricing of natural and produced resources. Where the resources were widely owned or controlled by individuals, the problem would appear solved, except for those who did not own and, also except for the fact that much consumption is of a collective nature—social insurance, parks, schools—and taxation would be required to make it possible. Where the natural and produced resources were owned by a small group in the social economy a fairly equal division of claims on goods could be accomplished only by taxation and a redivision through the state furnishing goods for collective consumption. If the non-human resources are collectively owned the consumption of goods can be approximately equalized through collective consumption.

4. The pricing of human resources may be varied in so far as social arrangement cannot equalize the marginal-money-products of the different types of human effort. However, it must be admitted that it is very difficult to discover the actual marginal money-products of many types of human effort simply because they are so inextricably bound up with other resources in production. Perhaps the pricing of it may be arbitrary as long as individuals are given those tasks which they appear to perform best. Even if the contribution of individuals who have an exceptional biological inheritance could be measured, it would be difficult to determine whether society is obligated to give them exceptional incomes as a reward for exceptional service. Codes of ethics must be relied upon to settle such matters.

There is a basis, perhaps, for variation in the prices of different forms of human effort when it is used in order to encourage individuals to become trained for important tasks and to strive to be more and more effective in economic activity. Every social economy is likely to use the stimulus of a greater individual claim on goods for greater or more important activity, in so far as it does not interfere with even more important social objectives—such as making a democratic society impossible of attainment. Even here the obligation of society is not clear for the inheritance is a gift of human culture, though the individual strove to acquire it.

These aspects of the problem seem to lead to the conclusion that the pricing of goods and resources to enable effective apportionment and combination in production is a distinct and separate problem from dividing the claims on the goods produced among the members of the social economy for consumption. Not only are there two separate problems involved but the institutional framework or social arrangements must provide for the division and use of claims in such a manner as will tend to accomplish social objectives before production can possibly be socially effective; otherwise the socially most needed goods cannot and will not be produced through the use of a pricing process.

BALANCING PRODUCTION AND CONSUMPTION THROUGH THE PRICING PROCESS

Keeping the flow of production and consumption equal at the maximum physical output of goods is a function of the pricing process and the environment in which it operates. A breakdown in the economic process might logically be a consequence of pricing rather than of any shortcomings of the money system, which merely reflects economic interrelationships. Indeed the place of a money system in the economic process can be easily over-emphasized. Its management might conceivably have a very disastrous effect on the organization of production and consumption through either inflation or deflation but it is by no means the only possible cause of changing price levels and maladjustment.

Any social economy which permits production units or industries to restrict output for the purpose of keeping up the price of goods and thus avoiding the necessity of repricing certain resources is bound to have breakdowns in the economic process because the unemployment resulting from restricted output decreases the volume of claims available for purchasing the output of other industries. The source of difficulty here is in the restriction of output and is not monetary in any real sense, because the money claims on output arise out of the use of resources.

Any social economy which permits (through a speculative mania) the prices of resources to get out of line with their actual marginal-money-products and then, further, permits the resources with inflated prices to become the basis for the creation of money claims on other goods and resources, may expect fluctuating price levels and maladjustments in the economic process.

Any social economy which permits the organization of production units to produce large volume of goods without at the same time providing for claims on goods to get into the hands of those who have the physical capacity for consumption may expect a maladjustment between the flow of resources into production and the flow of goods into consumption.

Classification of the Essential Functions of Organized Economic Units

The coördination of economic activities requires the establishment of arrangements and procedures for the performance of essential functions through whatever organized unit can most effectively get the desired results. The technology used and the objectives desired will determine the nature and scope of the essential functions. A high degree of interdependence between persons and areas is characteristic of a society using a machine technology and it necessitates the performance of these functions through economic units of increasing size and complexity. Where the provision of a high level of material well-being for every member of society is desired the economic process will have to be deliberately directed to that end.

Functions of Socio-Economic Units

A social economy, as a group of interdependent and coöperating individuals working toward common goals and subject in some degree to the same economic, political, and other institutions, appears to be the organized unit which may properly perform certain broad economic functions. By and through its institutional framework provision is made in some fashion for the following:

1. The relative quantities and qualities of the various resource units in so far as they are subject to social control.
2. The degree of the division of labor within and between socio-economic units.
3. A money system.
4. A procedure for pricing goods and resources.
5. Methods and procedures for controlling resources in their utilization and for claiming their imputed products.
6. Procedures for the discovery of new and improved types of goods for consumption.
7. The procedures and arrangements for organizing, managing, and coördinating production units and industries.

ECONOMIC FUNCTIONS OF A PRODUCTION UNIT

In attempting to secure a socially effective combination of resources, those who control production units will:

1. Select according to effectiveness and price resource units in such quantities as will result in production with the least-resource-cost.
2. Operate at the least-money-cost combination except where price and production policies temporarily necessitate production beyond that point.
3. Reprice non-shiftable resources to whatever extent is necessary to keep them in continuous operation.
4. Maintain an accounting system which can be used as a basis for a comparison of the relative effectiveness of the various production units as well as to determine the least-money-cost combination.
5. Perhaps discover and introduce new and improved techniques and processes in production and new and improved goods for consumption.

ECONOMIC FUNCTIONS OF AN INDUSTRIAL UNIT

The industry, consisting of those production units which contribute to the making of a particular good or, in a narrower sense, which make a particular contribution to the production of a good, appears to have a proper sphere of activity as an organized unit if certain additional economic functions are to be performed. It would:

1. Adjust the number of production units so that an output will tend to be produced which will be claimed by consumers at a price that will equal the cost at the least-cost combination.

2. Determine the price and output policies for the production units as a group when changes occur in the needs of consumers or in the cost of production.

3. Perhaps provide for the discovery of new and improved processes and techniques in production and of new and improved goods for consumption.

4. Direct the adoption and spread of new processes and techniques throughout the industry.

The performance of essential economic functions requires decisions based upon two types of measurements. One type is based upon physical standards furnished by the natural sciences; the other is based upon social standards. The physical engineers can determine the proper size and location of the production units and industries if a given volume of output is to be maintained using resources with specific money costs. On the other hand, to social engineers falls the task of creating an institutional framework through which social effectiveness in production, distribution, and consumption may be attained in the highest possible degree. Because the division of labor has become so pervasive, and individuals and groups are consequently so interdependent, centralization and specialization in the performance of economic functions seem inevitable. If the material well-being is to be maximized as an essential basis for the creation of a democratic society, the physical and social engineers will have to perform these functions toward that end rather than in the selfish interest of particular individuals or groups.

Part III. Instrumental Economics

Chapter XI
Economics: Science, Method, and Art

ECONOMICS IS A SOCIAL SCIENCE

A SCIENCE may be defined as systematized knowledge about a particular type or types of phenomena. Man is able to exert some control over the elements in his environment because it is possible to discover *causal relationships*. Sufficient heat *causes* water to expand until it vaporizes or becomes steam; the expansion process can be harnessed to turn dynamos which make electrical energy available. In trying to explain these very important processes in a machine technology scientists soon reach the unknown in "causes" and "properties"; for example, they simply do not know *why* atoms behave as they do. But the unknown is not reached in the natural sciences before it is possible to develop the present machine technology. So it is with economics as a social science. It is impossible to know and to systematize every aspect of economic activity but it is believed that enough can be known to permit a deliberate control over it in order to accomplish social purposes. The origin of the accepted concepts of needs for goods may not be explainable, but it is possible to explain why the output of goods per person is smaller in some regions than in others, so that the factors which influence the output can be controlled sufficiently to get more goods.

However, economics is not a science in the sense that physics, chemistry, and biology are sciences. The social environment which forms the background of economics as a science is constantly changing, while the natural order of the physical sciences does not change perceptibly. The human nature that is biological has not changed in thousands of years but the human nature that is a social inheritance changes constantly. It is because of this shifting background that economics cannot be confined to the study of the characteristics and operation of a particular economic order. That is why it is a social science.

TYPES OF ECONOMIC LAWS

Knowledge in the form of generalizations about economic activity constitutes a science. Such generalizations, principles, tendencies, or laws may be grouped into three classes.

One class is really based on the natural sciences and would be as applicable to the society of a primitive tribe as to a machine civilization. For example, in the utilization of resources there is a universal tendency for the average number of bushels per worker to decline sooner or later as more and more workers try to produce wheat on a given acre of land. In the consumption of goods it is also universally true that as an individual attempts to consume more and more apples at a particular time he will not attach equal importance to the desirability of the first and the tenth considering the other things he might eat or the other ways he could use his time. The same would also be true of groups in collective consumption. These laws are based upon the observation that there are physical limitations to the capacity of a given acre of land to produce wheat and physical and psychological limits to the individual's or group's capacity to consume apples or any other good. Laws of this type are comparable with those of the natural sciences; they would be useful as a starting point in the analysis of a certain situation regardless of the characteristics of the existing economic order. Both were used as basic generalizations in the analysis of the principles of social effectiveness in resource utilization.

A second class of economic generalizations rests upon such assumptions as a given set of social objectives or a given level of technology, but is independent of a particular economic order. It is customary to accept as a principle the generalization that a large output per person is desirable, but that is based upon the assumption that the society is some sort of a democracy. A society ruled by an aristocracy may not be at all interested in such matters—in fact a relatively small output per person might be more desirable from the point of view of the aristocrats. It is also customary to accept the generalization that the performance of specialized tasks by persons and regions will increase the total output but that also depends upon the stage of technology assumed; specialization is made possible by improvements in technology and consequently the extent to which it can be carried and still increase the output of goods per person depends upon the extent of scientific knowledge. Generalizations of this type form a background for the study of any economic order but they are useful only if the assumed conditions are realistic. In this analysis of basic economic principles and functions it was assumed that a democratic society was desirable and that a machine technology was available for use. The first and second classes of generalizations have been the exclusive subject matter of this analysis.

A third class of economic generalizations rests upon the assumption of the existence of particular institutions and social arrangements for organizing economic activity and consists of observations about their interrelationships and interactions. For example, it is thought that if a great many people, who are able to do so, suddenly decide to purchase a certain good instead of other goods that they have been buying, the price of that good will rise and the prices of other goods will fall. But there are significant assumptions behind such a "law." It is assumed that the good is being sold under market arrangements whereby the sellers are permitted to get as high a price as they can instead of only the money cost of production. It is assumed also that other goods will continue to be produced in about the same quantities as before. Such a law is useful only when the conditions assumed actually exist.

Laws or generalizations of all three types are based upon observation and experimentation and many of them are outright truisms. They are used as a starting point in the analysis of a given situation but that is all. They are not a set of axioms on how to organize economic activity. Many people seem to think that such institutions as private property, along with the competitive organization of economic activity, is justified by economic laws. This is emphatically not the case; in fact, the study of economic theory may show that such institutions are actually detrimental to the attainment of social effectiveness in the utilization of resources. Likewise, those who hold that price-fixing by governmental agencies is undesirable because it is a violation of the "laws of supply and demand" are utterly misconceiving the nature of such laws. Actually a proper understanding of the conditions with respect to demand and supply will enable the price-fixing agency to do its work well.

Economics is a social science in the sense that it attempts to explain the theory of resource utilization and the functional and structural organization of economic activity in such a manner that man will be able through adequate control to accomplish social objectives. Such control will depend upon the possibility of obtaining sufficient knowledge to build the various parts of economic order as bridges, skyscrapers, drill presses, and dirigibles are built—according to a premeditated plan.

Certain aspects of the analogy between building a bridge and building a part of an economic order are pertinent. A bridge is built with the materials most available and suitable at the place and time it is needed and for the specific purpose it is required to serve. The nature of the terrain and the subsoil will determine the materials most suitable and the method and procedure to be followed in construction. So it is with the building of any part of an economic order.

THE SCIENTIFIC METHOD IN ECONOMICS

The building of an economic order by deliberate planning is not so simple as building a bridge, however. Three groups of persons are interested in changes in an economic order: One group will look forward to changes with the expectation that their well-being will be enhanced as a result; another group will view change with alarm because it will mean a limitation on activities that were considered important and beneficial privileges; a third group will attempt to predict the consequences of particular changes and to suggest methods of bringing about changes to accomplish particular objectives. This third group includes the social scientists, among them the economists, but it must not be forgotten that as members of society each of us is also a member of or sympathetic with one of the other groups. Planning an economic order in a democratic society must inevitably take the form of a social struggle between groups which can be resolved only through the pressure of common social objectives and attitudes.

The student of economic activity is therefore faced with the task of dealing with problems which arouse intense emotions and prejudices. Furthermore, he faces constantly the task of making and using generalizations under continuously changing circumstances. Great difficulty is experienced in making generalizations accurately and even greater difficulty is met in using them only when they are appropriate.

Consequently great care must be exercised in observation and analysis. The term "scientific method" has been invoked to lend prestige to a procedure which appears to be a sensible and an intellectually honest attempt to arrive at conclusions regarding interrelationships and interactions in economic activity. Likewise the term "unscientific" has become the stigma attached to those conclusions which have been arrived at by a selection of data or bits of evidence which tend to substantiate only what it is desired to prove.

When controversies over socio-economic policies become heated, those who cannot scientifically or with intellectual honesty support their position not infrequently resort to the subterfuge of claiming that they are "practical" while those holding the opposing views are "theoretical."

Regardless of how practical a generalization may be it is nevertheless a theory, for a theory is merely an explanation.[1] A correct theory about the influence of import duties on the volume of foreign trade or on the real wages of a country, for example, is merely a true explanation. So many widely accepted theories about various interrelationships and interactions in economic activity are really inaccurate that anyone who doubts them is called a "theorist" in derision. Yet every generalization is based on theory because knowledge of natural and social phenomena is incomplete and the task of the social scientist is simply to try to formulate accurate theories honestly based on an intelligent interpretation of the pertinent information available and verified by the opinions of others, if not by actual experience.

An individual may hold to inaccurate theories not only because he is ignorant, or because he does not wish to go to the

[1] A hypothesis is a provisional conjecture as to causes or relations of phenomena; a theory is a verified hypothesis applicable to many related phenomena.

trouble of doing his own thinking, but because he may want to believe that something is true. It is ironic that certain individuals should argue that import duties on particular goods are essential to the maintenance of high "wages" in a country and at the same time hold that import duties are necessary because money costs in the country are higher than elsewhere due to higher wages. Such statements are quite inaccurate but many individuals believe what is convenient to serve their particular interests and they are, of course, unscientific. As new social objectives are adopted or new technology is developed, new social policies of a political and economic nature are suggested and indeed become inevitable. Principles and laws based upon the old objectives or technology must be discarded, but in the struggle to change the economic order to make it conform to the new conditions, the new generalizations are likely to be called "theoretical" and the old "practical."

Except for those based on the natural sciences, generalizations about economic acivity fit only the particular situation assumed. Those who theorize about such matters as the influence of import duties on wages will have to use judgment or "common sense" in selecting and weighing the facts that can be observed. Individuals may come to quite different conclusions if they select different facts or give those selected different weight.

AS AN ART

Before pertinent facts can be selected and a sensible weight given to them it will be necessary to know what purpose the theory is to serve. In formulating economic theory contemporary social objectives, attitudes, and philosophies must be considered. Such theory then becomes useful in determining socio-economic policies. It is in the formulation of policies to fit a given set of circumstances that economics becomes an art. Perhaps it would be better described as an art using the scientific method to discover socially desirable procedure in utilizing resources.[2] Perhaps it is more of an art than a science. Its place as an art is aptly described in the following statement:

[2] An art is knowledge applied and made efficient by skill.

The economist, as such, is not qualified to set up social objectives. Economic objectives are not in themselves the highest motives in life. Neither individual nor national wealth and riches constitutes a sufficient end in itself. The economist is not even qualified to say what distribution of the continuously produced stream of finished consumer goods and services should be made among the people in the best interests of social justice. Given some such utilitarian objective as the maximization of the national income, or the greatest economic good to the greatest number, the economist is qualified to assist with economic plans and tools which may lead more quickly and effectively to the stated objective.[3]

Economics, as a science, method, and art, is social in outlook and cannot be impartial in the sense that economists may ignore the social consequences of particular aspects of the organization of economic activity. We must agree heartily with one social scientist who writes concerning his own work:

I have no apology to make for the method of presentation in this work nor for the "partisanship" with which I may be charged. This book frankly advocates social insurance as a feasible method of social security. In the presentation of the data I have been forced to give prominence to those factors which are crucial to this issue. The writer on social problems cannot possibly record all the facts. He must definitely select those which are of major importance and discard minor details.

Nor can I accept the doctrine, so widely prevalent a few years ago, that writers on economic and social problems should be "objective" and "impartial" and have no point of view of their own. The function of the student of social problems is not that of a technician observing and recording social phenomena with inhuman detachment. If he is worth his salt, he cannot assume the calm aloofness of the physicist and biologist in their laboratories. Such mimicry of the physical sciences, inspired by some of our academicians and "research" foundations, all too often financed and directed by persons vitally concerned in the preservation of the *status quo,* has been largely responsible for the passive and uncritical acceptance of the economic fantasies of our generation. Social phenomena were isolated and so treated as to impede understanding and make impossible significant interpretation. Facts were not evaluated in terms of their social implications, but merely recorded in heavy, lifeless tomes. A spurious impartiality was built up, and every discussion began with "on the one hand," and ended with "on the other hand." Economic and social writing became the

[3] R. L. Meghell and R. H. Barrett, "The Economics of Social Justice," in the Springfield *Daily Republican,* Feb. 14, 1934.

art, to use the eloquent phrase of Professor Walton Hamilton of Yale University, of "setting down propositions in which the nouns give and the adjectives take away."

The times cry for critical insight and a true evaluation of social forces. Complicated statistical tables and elaborate correlations must not be allowed to obstruct logic and common sense. The realistic presentation of essential facts, the discovery of their import, and the elaboration of far-sighted, constructive programs are the true functions of social science.[4]

[4] Abraham Epstein, *Insecurity, a Challenge to America*, Foreword.

Chapter XII

The Background of Economics Today

SOCIAL ENGINEERING

DURING the past century man has increased his control over the elements and forces of nature tremendously. A powered-machine technology has become possible. During the next century it appears probable that man will try to make just as tremendous changes in the social organization so that the new physical powers may be fully utilized to promote the social wellbeing. Engineers, who have mastered the natural sciences, today direct the construction of bridges, dams, highways, buildings, ships, and machines of countless variety superior to any human activity has previously produced. Perhaps engineers who have mastered the social sciences will in the future construct socioeconomic organizations superior to any in the present or the past. Social engineering may become an integral part of human activity. If it does it will be a result of a definite shift in the generally accepted ideas concerning the nature of human society and the social process.

The dynamic factors which determine the characteristics of an economic order at a particular period in human history are ever in the process of change. The social objectives in economic activity, the dominant ideas with respect to the proper method of organizing it and the natural and technological environments interact upon each other and bring forth an ecoomic order that is in harmony with the particular environment. Economics is, of course, a product of the same dynamic factors. So impressively does the background of economics change that it seems logical to describe the economics of the passing economic order and the economics of the emerging economic order.

THE ECONOMICS OF THE PASSING ECONOMIC ORDER

It is apparent, when the dominant institutions and beliefs of a few decades ago are examined, that the nature of economic laws and the uses to which they are put depends very much upon the social philosophy which furnishes the rational basis for a particular method of organizing economic activity. The following paragraphs present a brief description of the socio-economic arrangements and beliefs which have been dominant for a century or more in the United States:

Our economic system is generally conceived and characterized as "capitalistic." This means that industry consists of privately owned individual units; each organized and operated for its own advantage; each striving to make maximum profits through monetary or price transactions. Certain special industries are regulated in various respects for the general protection of the public, but for the most part each individual unit in each industry is free to carry out its own policies in competition with other units and other industries. Each expands its activities as it can, keeps its costs down as low as possible, and seeks the highest return obtainable from the sale of its products. This may be regarded as a competitive price-profit system.

Up to comparatively recent years, the rather prevailing assumption has been that the competitive forces within private business furnish a comprehensive system of self-adjustment so that each industry, each unit or each class receives benefits proportionate to its efficiency and contribution to the total output, through the process of gradual or "marginal" adjustment. Competition has been supposed to effect automatically a balanced allocation of capital funds to the development of the various industries and their individual units, and proper compensation of the respective elements engaged in production and distribution. The forces of competition were conceived as underlying economic law which determined capital expansion, production, prices, wages, interest and profits. They were regarded as self-operative. Any material interference through government or otherwise would not only be futile but would result in public injury rather than welfare.[1]

Another paragraph emphasizes some additional points:

Society is composed of individuals, each struggling to avoid pain and to secure pleasure-giving goods. Where legal freedom of contract and of motion exists, the individual applies his talents and capital to the enterprise for which he is best fitted. Competition guarantees the survival of those who render economical services at the lowest price. The purchaser of the goods knows what is best for himself and can avoid adulterations and frauds. Competition and rent regulate prices, profits, and wages so that each productive factor in society—land, labor, and capital—obtains a reward fairly apportioned to its deserts.

[1] John Bauer and Nathaniel Gold, *Permanent Prosperity and How to Get It*, pp. 2-3. (Harper and Brothers, 1934).

Pressure of population keeps wages near the cost of subsistence, and the improvidence of the poor assures an abundant labor supply. Everybody is the best judge of what is beneficial to himself and by trusting to his instincts and reason will find the place in society to which his merits entitle him. Attempts to control prices, wages, and the quality of goods are interferences with natural laws, bound to fail and to injure those for whose supposed benefit they are made.[2]

These beliefs are still tenaciously held in undiluted form by many contemporary thinkers, one of whom asks:

Who can doubt that there are natural laws in the social and economic as well as in the physical world, and that these cannot be overridden without courting disaster? The law of supply and demand, for example, cannot be thwarted by governmental price-fixing or even by experiments with the currency. Those who bite on that rock are sure to break their teeth. Just as incontrovertible is the axiomatic truth that men live in this world only by exchanging their labor, or the fruits of it, for the labor and products of other men. . . . Wisdom in government, I submit, consists in discovering these natural laws and following them—not in devising hasty experiments whereby they may be circumvented.[3]

He implies that there are economic laws which are "natural" in the sense that they indicate how economic activity should be organized regardless of social objectives or technology.

These quotations have briefly characterized the economic order inherited by the twentieth century. It was labeled economic "liberalism" in contrast with the preceding economic order dominated by "mercantilism" in which chartered monopolies for carrying on certain economic activities were common and in which much economic activity was carefully regulated through the state to promote the interests of particular groups and to enhance the power and glory of the nation. Economic liberalism implies a negative liberty for all but a positive liberty for those who wield economic power through control over resources.

It is significant that the spirit of economic liberalism developed in a period of great colonization and expansion of trade, when agriculture was still the dominant occupation, when manufacturing was carried on in the home or in small shops and

[2] Charles A. Beard, "The Political Heritage of the Twentieth Century," *Yale Review*, Spring, 1929, pp. 466-67.
[3] John W. Davis, in *New York Times*, March 4, 1934, 4:7.

when the volume of goods produced above the needs for actual subsistence was very small. Perhaps even more significant is the fact that it developed in the period when the natural sciences were developing rapidly and the theories of evolution and the survival of the fittest dominated man's thinking.

Now the scene appears to have shifted for one of our most illustrious historians believes that:

> The fundamental stock of ideas and political institutions inherited by the twentieth century was created in the image of handicrafts and agriculture, petty production and marginal subsistence—and has little, if any, relevance to the fact patterns and immense potentialities brought into the world by science and the machine.[4]

THE ECONOMICS OF THE EMERGING ECONOMIC ORDER

Certain changes during the past few decades have been tremendously dynamic in their impact upon the economic order. The use of inanimate energy has increased with astounding rapidity as a consequence of the development of scientific knowledge. In order to harness and use this energy, machines and other forms of produced resources have become essential, ever changing in form and ever increasing in volume. The consequent flow of consumption goods from the production processes is aptly described as larger and larger "mass." Somehow consumers must have the opportunity to consume this mass flow. That needed coördination between the capacity to produce and the opportunity to consume constitutes a problem of major importance in a society using machine technology. Abundance as well as scarcity characterizes a machine civilization.

The use of inanimate power and the vast agglomeration of machines and other produced resources has made the organization of large production units coördinated into far flung industries essential in attaining a least-money-cost combination.

Both production and consumption goods are moved long distance for utilization and consumption. Vast agglomerations of resources, including thousands of persons, are combined in a single production process. Persons and areas have become interdependent as they diffused, causing frequent and serious maladjustment even on a world-wide scale. Maladjustment results

[4] Beard, *op. cit.*, p. 479.

in idle resources and in unused potential capacity to produce goods.

A delicate balance between production and consumption must, therefore, be maintained while the processes of both production and consumption must be made to conform to contemporary social objectives and attitudes. The failure to maintain this balance in a satisfactory degree appears to be due to the fact that the different dynamic factors have not changed in a synchronized fashion. Especially have social attitudes toward the proper methods of organizing economic activity lagged behind changes in social objectives and in technology. Consequently the feeling that the methods and institutions which are being used to organize economic activity are today unequal to their task has become widespread.

Furthermore, the urge to create a democratic society has not abated. A group of philosophers and historians hold that it is still to be recognized as the dominant social objective:

Especially significant, as a conditioning factor in American life, is the well-established national tradition of government and society based on the ideals of popular democracy and of personal liberty and dignity —that tradition that government is organized solely for the purpose of promoting the highest welfare of the governed, collectively and individually, that in all great divisions of economy, administration, and culture the interests of the masses of the people are to be considered paramount, and that, since every person is of moral worth and dignity in himself, no man, woman or child can be exploited by another without doing violence to the essential spirit of American democracy and liberty. This is a tradition so strong and, in the opinion of the Commission, so authentic and valid that, despite academic criticisms, despite assaults by selfish or predatory groups, it may be expected to give direction to the further evolution of life and institutions in the United States.[5]

If it is true that "the nature of the economic system we have depends largely upon the mass thinking upon it,"[6] then

[5] From the report of the American Historical Association's Commission on the Social Studies in the Schools, *Conclusions and Recommendations*, p. 12. (Charles Scribners' Sons, 1934).

[6] "'I hold very strongly (as against a certain school of economic historians) that the thing which really determines the nature of the economic system we have depends largely upon mass thinking upon it." J. L. Hammond, "The Basis of British Industrial Life," in *British Labor Speaks*.

the key to the general nature of the emerging order and the place of economics in it will be the attitudes and beliefs which are now becoming generally accepted. Perhaps the following list contains the most significant of them:

1. Human nature, as a conditioning factor in the economic order, is a social rather than a biological inheritance.
2. Society is "a growing whole."
3. The economic order is man-made and economic laws are generalizations which are helpful in attaining social objectives through it.
4. The proper functions of the state are whatever will promote the well-being of the people.

HUMAN NATURE

Human nature does not require the existence of a particular economic order. During the centuries of recorded history, social arrangements for carrying on economic activity have changed constantly and widely. But biological human nature has not changed.

At least fifty thousand years ago man was able to stand erect; his free hand with its apposite thumb was usable as a tool-grasping and later a tool-making member; his voice box had apparently its present-day plasticity; his muscular powers were, if anything, greater than our own; the quality of his brain cells—his native brain power—was apparently the equal of our own. Since no essential changes have taken place in man's biological make-up in the last fifty thousand years or more we have come to think of this element as unchanging, as a fixed datum.

So also we have come to regard man's natural environment as unchanging. . . .

If, then, there has been upon this earth approximately the same kind of biological man for the last fifty thousand years or more, and if for an even longer period of time there have been substantially no changes in natural resources and powers, it follows that the great difference in man's status today as compared with his status of fifty thousand years ago is to be ascribed to that human product, that factor which man himself has brought into being—culture.[7]

[7] Leon C. Marshall, "The Changing Economic Order," *The Annals of the American Academy of Political and Social Science*, 147, 1.

During the thousands of years that "biological man" and "natural resources and powers" have been constant factors there has been a countless variety of social arrangements for solving the basic economic problems. Human nature as a biological inheritance is apparently adaptable to a variety of economic orders. Yet it must be biological human nature that has caused change. Man has built culture. New objectives, attitudes, and knowledge have always kept human society in a state of flux.

The human nature that is a social inheritance is the conditioning factor in a particular economic order. Much of what any individual is results from his social inheritance, that is, from the influence of the environment upon his beliefs, skills, and knowledge; but by using his imagination an individual may constantly add to and re-evaluate his inheritance. His resulting human nature is not a constant but is "infinitely diverse, infinitely malleable, infinitely subject to change."

We cannot speak, therefore, with great assurance of a "natural propensity of men to truck and barter." They might have under certain circumstances an equal propensity to steal or to give things away.

It must not be assumed, however, that the human nature which is a social inheritance can be too easily changed. Every individual is early inculcated through his family and group associations with a particular set of attitudes, beliefs, and loyalties to which he generally holds very tenaciously throughout his life. He learns the rational basis of the various institutions and practices of his environment, and even though they may have long since ceased to function effectively, he may profess to believe that they do—as long as he and his immediate associates are not affected adversely. With the contemporary means of communication, including the press and the radio, the opinions of vast numbers of people may possibly be changed rather quickly. If so, change in the economic order may be more rapid than in past generations.

We may conclude, therefore, that

the bulk of our human behavior is acquired or learned rather than inborn. Some of our traits are acquired universally, the result of certain universal experiences and conditions, others are acquired personally, as a result of experiences peculiar to individuals, and others are acquired culturally, as a result of a particular culture in which we have been reared. . . . The only hope of making culture surely better for man . . . is through social invention.[8]

THE NATURE OF HUMAN SOCIETY

Society is not just a collection of individuals, each having a full understanding of what will promote his and the social wellbeing, a free will to obtain it, and a personal responsibility for his own acts and their consequences.[9] It has just been pointed out that the individual is largely a product of his cultural environment. A society is rather a group of individuals integrated through a somewhat similar biological and social inheritance by means of social arrangements for organizing economic and other activities. We may think of human society as "one growing whole, unified by ceaseless currents of interaction, but at the same time differentiated into those diverse forms of energy which we see as men, factions, tendencies, doctrines and institutions."[10]

While society is a "growing whole" it does not follow a cultural order pattern because any particular society is made up of "diverse forms of energy" that are constantly changing and consequently causing a continually shifting pattern of organization. It is in deliberately moulding "men, factions, tendencies, doctrines, and institutions" that intelligence and knowledge are used to obtain the kind of economic order that will give the desired results. This idea of achieving social objectives by controlling and even planning an economic order in considerable detail has been widely accepted only in recent years.

In this view of society as something of an organism some conflict between persons and groups, over places of power, prestige, and possibly goods, is regarded as inevitable but it is a conflict which need not be brutal, cruel, or wasteful. It is a conflict tempered by the pressure of common objectives and in-

---
[8] Folsom, *op. cit.*
[9] "The popular impression that nothing important can take place in human life without the human will being at the bottom of it is an illusion as complete as the old view that the universe revolved about our planet." Cooley, *op. cit.*, p. 15.
[10] *Ibid.*, pp. 3-4.

terests and by the inculcation of individuals with a social conscience and responsibility. It is, perhaps, another mark of civilization that conflict, except war, is to some extent carried on with less brutality and its circumscribing is one field of human activity in which intelligence has been used with some success.

Nor does this view imply that every society passes through the life-cycle stages of a biological organism. The analogy between society and the plant and animal structure is not carried that far. There is no definite law of growth and decay which enables us to predict the fate of a particular society. Conflict between individuals and groups does not inevitably lead to decay or to cyclical change. Civilizations do not inevitably decay; they may simply develop new, but still temporary, characteristics; they never reach a completely static condition.

THE ECONOMIC ORDER AND ECONOMICS

The economic order is not, therefore, "natural" but man-made. Economic generalizations are not fixed laws on the proper methods of organizing economic activity at any time or place, but are rather scientific explanations of particular economic phenomena that are helpful in organizing resource utilization if appropriate with respect to time and place. To put the point strongly:

> That the economic system is controlled by fixed laws is no longer believed by most intelligent people. It is a product of man and can be changed by man through proper thought and means as may appear desirable.
>
> The assumption of "natural" laws in the economic field, with their automatic and beneficent operation in the interest of individuals and the public at large, has been extensively discarded by economists and is now advanced only by the naive or by those who have special interests in being left alone as against the welfare of the public at large.[11]

But can the economic order be deliberately changed? Can we actually learn enough about the social process to greatly influence the course of events? Perhaps to a considerable degree, though it is not likely that man will ever have sufficient knowledge to explain all social change and to direct in detail the manner and time of its appearance. Significant changes may

[11] Bauer and Gold, *op. cit.*, pp. 3, 4.

take place before many members of a society are aware of them; social groups may at all times do other than they intend; yet there is a widespread belief that knowledge and intelligence may play a very important part in shaping social and economic organization. There has developed a belief in their efficacy as aids in obtaining an economic order that will accomplish the prevailing social objectives. This belief, known as instrumental philosophy, is described by Bertrand Russell who suggests its origin and its meaning:

> The philosophy inspired by industrialism is seeping away the static conception of knowledge which dominated both medieval and modern philosophy, and has substituted what it calls the Instrumental Theory, the very name of which is suggested by machinery. In the Instrumental Theory, there is not a single state of mind which consists of knowing a truth—there is a way of acting, a manner of handling the environment, which is appropriate, and whose appropriateness constitutes what alone can be called knowledge as these philosophers understand it. One might sum up this theory by a definition: *To know something is to be able to change it as we wish.* There is no place in this outlook for the beatific vision, nor for any notion of final excellence.[12]

So economics becomes one of the instruments for constantly improving the economic order. The nature and extent of change depends upon certain conditioning factors, of which the most important appear to be the existence of individual leaders with intelligence and imagination, the level of the culture of the group, and the character of the ideas which are in circulation in the group. The preceding paragraphs have suggested some of the recent changes in the level of culture and in the ideas which are in circulation in our generation that make possible the development of a new economical order. But new ideas may not be readily accepted. Suggested changes in the objectives and methods of economic organization cannot well be demonstrated as successful, like an invention of a technical nature. That is why an individual who invents a new economic order, or even a small part of one, is looked upon with suspicion. At one time technical inventions were considered machinations of the devil but attitudes have changed regarding such matters. Perhaps in-

---

[12] Bertrand Russell, "Science" in *Whither Mankind*, p. 72. Edited by Charles A. Beard (Longmans, Green & Co., 1929).

novation in the economic order may come to be regarded more highly, if, indeed, it is not already.

New ways of organizing economic activity must first appear in the imagination of some individual who has been in some manner stimulated to give his attention to the matter. While he may be convinced that his "invention" is a good one he must convince others either by persuasion or by demonstration that it is so. This process of cultural change is described as follows:

> Here, then, is the method of cultural evolution. Certain steps in the process stand out clearly: 1. The creation under the spur of some crisis of new patterns of action, by means of imagination and reasoning, utilizing the materials of the physical and social environment and to some extent also instinctive impulses and psychic accidents. These new patterns of action are usually formed by some individual in the group of exceptional attainments—a leader. 2. The diffusion of this new pattern of action throughout the group by means of imitation and communication, with ultimate acceptance by the group if it is found useful. The new pattern of action thus becomes a social or cultural pattern or trait. 3. Social patterns thus adopted become embodied in the social traditions of the group and so a part of its culture. All knowledge, beliefs, values, and standards which the group finds useful, or believes to be useful, are thus embodied in the group tradition. There is in the group, however, not one tradition, but many; as many as there are interests and arts of life. 4. The final step in the cultural process comes in the inculcation of the social tradition in the young through some system of social education.[13]

In every organized society the state, as a sovereign authority, is an agency which both prevents and causes change. Individuals and groups who are able to wield the power of the state may use that power to reshape the arrangements, customs or institutions which influence the activity of the people, or the power of the state may be used to suppress all innovation.

THE PLACE OF THE STATE

The place of the state in economic activity has been a moot question in recent generations. There has been a tendency to look upon it as an organization apart from its citizens and as having interests which conflicted with theirs. Perhaps the acceptance of this idea of a conflict of interest has been due partly

[13] Charles A. Elwood, *Cultural Change*, pp. 48-49. (Century Co., 1927).

to a continuation of the sentiment created by the struggle to overthrow an hereditary ruling class, and partly to the fact that governments which perform the functions of the state often favor the interests of particular groups more than those of others. This attitude is reflected in the following question:

> In all historical development we see the interaction of two great sets of forces. On the one hand there are the forces from below, the forces of spontaneity, of germination. On the other hand, there are the forces from above, the forces of authority, of formulation. Speaking very broadly, we may express one set of forces by the term society, and the other set by the term state. We may put our question thus: Which ought to possess the dominant influence over the other—society or the state?[14]

The question is not satisfactorily put, for a state is actually an organized society; there should be no real question of dominance in a democracy since that is supposed to be a government "of the people, by the people, and for the people." Indeed, the strength of the "forces from below" depends upon the action of capable, energetic, intelligent individuals. If each individual has the actual opportunity to develop his capacities and to use them when once developed, these forces will be as powerful "spontaneous and germinating" as they can be made. But the state is the agency through which individuals are offered such opportunities. If the state does not set up common rules for activity, conflict between individuals and groups soon results in a stratified society in which large elements of the population are denied the opportunity to really become spontaneous and germinating forces.

It has been customary to attribute the spontaneous forces in economic activity during recent centuries to the free play of the gain or selfish motive. This is probably not the case. A broadening of the opportunities of the mass of the people to develop and use their capacities individually and collectively seems a truer explanation of accelerated economic development. This has been largely a result of the assumption by the state of the responsibility for enlarging the opportunities of a larger number of the citizens; especially has the state broadened the opportunity to get, use, and advance scientific knowledge.

[14] George Unwin, *Studies in Economic History*, p. 28.

While the state is the pervasive and sovereign institution in a society the fact must not be ignored that the government, which is the set of individuals operating the political mechanism, is controlled by those who gain and retain their power in accordance with a special set of rules. Governments reflect and compromise the conflicting interests of various groups in society. To be democratic a government must be organized under a set of rules which permits representation of all conflicting groups and it must so circumscribe the activities of all individuals and groups that social objectives will be attained. The degree and nature of the conflicts which the state must curb depend upon the nature of the economic organization, for example, the existence of private property results in conflicts between owners and non-owners, debtors and creditors, landlords and tenants, and employers and employees which the state must somehow mitigate through the establishment of common rules of action. The elimination of the sources of conflict may become one of the major duties of the state in a machine civilization.

A president of the American economic Association recently spoke as follows:

We must recognize that both individual and social adjustment is the result of common effort. Although we can reconcile the achievement of individual ends with the welfare of society as a whole, it does not follow that general welfare can be achieved without positive thought and effort, as a mere residual consequence of the enlightened selfishness of individuals. It is no longer possible to accept any concept of a mechanical self-regulating society that excludes the state as an agency of change. The state must need be an active participant in social process.[15]

The importance of social objectives in furnishing the basis for state policies cannot be over-emphasized. Social objectives weld a society together, making it possible to curb the powers and privileges of some members while extending those of others. Long established customs, traditions, and institutions in the economic organization are swept away by governments if those

[15] Abbot Payson Usher, "Liberal Theory of Constructive Statecraft." Presidential address delivered at the forty-sixth annual meeting of the American Economic Association. Printed in *American Economic Review*, March, 1934, p. 8.

in control are convinced that such arrangements are detrimental to the attainment of accepted social aims.

In a democratic society there can be no limit to the scope of the state's activity. Its function is to promote the well-being of the citizens in whatever manner that can be accomplished. The answer to the question—which ought to be dominant over the other society or the state?—is that they are two aspects of the same social unit. This view of the place of the state is clearly outlined in the following quotation:

> No province can be found which is absolutely that of the state, in the sense of excluding individual action, while equally there is no province of the isolated subject which absolutely excludes the government. The individual finds his sphere to be no narrower than the state itself, while the sphere of the government may be logically extended to embrace all the interests and actions of every man and woman. This is the theory of organic unity, which holds it absurd to draw a line between two things whose essential nature lies in their connection with each other.
>
> This may seem merely a theoretical answer to the problem, but it prepares the way for the only solution that will work in practice. No absolute barrier of any kind can be set up anywhere to the action of the government which has both a right and a duty to do everything the state entrusts it with; and the state must insist on government undertaking everything which will further its ultimate end, or any of its more immediate aims, legitimate in themselves and consistent with the final goal. The actual province of any government, then, is just whatever is entrusted to it by the sovereign legislature as the source of positive law. The ideal province is that which is best fitted to fulfill the final destiny (or what is the same thing, to realize the highest welfare) of the nation as a branch of the family of mankind. Its limits may thus shift from time to time and from country to country. No absolute boundaries or rules can be laid down *a priori*. The government ought to interfere in any place to which the sovereignty of the state extends, if the good it thus effects outweighs on the whole the evil. But in estimating such evil and good reference must be made to remote contingencies as well as near ones; a broad statesmanlike view must be taken, founded on a wide experience of affairs and on the principles of human nature as laid down by the most advanced science of the day.
>
> This solution of the problem, which is here taken to be the only sound one, differs from all the others. It differs . . . in condemning the policy of mere drifting with the current, without formulating principles of guidance and without listening to the voice of science. It

condemns the treatment of each case as an isolated problem, and the see-saw inconsistent policy that results—one thing straggling in one direction, while its fellow drifts in the other. Every act of policy must be ultimately judged by the final end of the state itself, and by those approved minor ends which political science has declared to be for the time consistent with, and conducive to, that higher goal. Thus a principle of order is introduced.

It also differs from the socialistic plan. For, though it concedes that the government may be lawfully and justly endowed with powers to do everything, it admits no absolute presumption in favour of community of property or of government interferences as opposed to private initiative.

It differs from individualism in refusing to admit the truth of any philosophy which would find man's highest good apart from his fellowmen, and because it refuses to admit any absolute limits to the action of the central authority acting for the good of the whole.

It differs from those who would effect a compromise between the last two theories, because it cannot admit any distinct province of the man apart from the state. It does not look on the government and the subject as two unconnected principles which approach each other from opposite sides, and it does not try to allocate the sum of human interests between them, settling by a contract or compromise that everything on this side of an imaginary line goes to the one party and everything on that side to the other.[16]

The widespread acceptance of this view of the functions of the state as a collective agent will not only tend to change profoundly the nature of the existing economic order but it will influence the approach to the study of economic activity, for the satisfactory solution of the basic economic problems may depend more and more upon extension of state functions as machine technology increases the interdependence of persons and areas.

It will mean that methods will have been subordinated to objectives and that social arrangements, customs, and traditions will be revered and retained only as they continue to serve useful social purposes. It will mean a recognition of truth in the following statement:

Man's cardinal error through all the ages has been his habit of regarding culture, or civilization, as a structure in which the parts exist for the whole. To liken the State, the Church, or other institution unto a great edifice, a great machine, or a great organism, presents indeed a

[16] W. S. McKechnie, *The State and the Individual*, pp. 167-68. (James MacLehose & Sons, Glascow, 1896).

captivating picture. But it is a misleading picture. We shall better perceive our destiny if we imagine civilization as a convenient framework for the development of the individual lives that live upon it, and not as an organism existing for its own sake. The test of a civilization is neither its "material greatness" nor yet its "spiritual achievement" in the sense usually implied. It is the long-run happiness of the people.[17]

SUMMARY STATEMENT ON CHANGING ATTITUDES

As scientific knowledge is extended and as social objectives with respect to individual and collective well-being expand needs, the operation of an existing economic order is examined more and more carefully to determine its effectiveness. Consequently the twentieth century is witnessing changes in attitudes regarding the best methods of organizing economic activity. These promise to be as great in degree and as pervasive as those which have occurred in technology and in standards of well-being. The nature, causes and magnitude of these changed attitudes are aptly summarized by an eminent economist:

A usual way of referring to such developments is to say that we are living in a régime of increasing governmental control—of increasing social control with particular reference to governmental control. That is, of course, true, and the reasons are not far to seek. We have become quite well convinced that the first fundamental assumption of the *laissez-faire* (economic liberalism) régime is false. This first assumption, you will remember, was that every individual of sound mind and mature age knows reasonably well his own self-interest. While this may be said to have been substantially true of the simpler society of the past, the kaleidoscopic changes of the last generation have made it highly improbable that every individual can know his own self-interest even reasonably well. The second assumption of the *laissez-faire* régime was that the individual will follow his self interest and in so doing will be led "as by an invisible hand" to promote the public welfare. This second assumption we can no longer grant; the last hundred years of history have furnished abundant evidence to the contrary. At the same time that we have lost our faith in the easy assumptions of the *laissez-faire* régime, we have been beckoned in the direction of increasing governmental intervention by several considerations. One is the fact that the increasing size and increasing complexity of our society have meant a tremendous increase in the number of points of contact and, hence, in the number of points of possible conflict—conflicts which, in the very nature of the case, must be adjudi-

---

[17] Folsom, *op. cit.*, p. 503.

cated. Then, too, we have come to be vastly more tolerant of governmental intervention than was the case two hundred years ago. It was one thing to be suspicious of government when the government was that of a despotic king; it is quite another thing to be suspicious of government (and we still have ample ground for a new kind of suspicion) when government means the rule of the people. In the same period that our hostility to government has declined, increasing scientific knowledge and scientifically established standards have opened wide the opportunity for governmental intervention in such matters as the regulation of public construction, the guaranty of purity of food supply, and so forth. Then, too, the coming in of the evolutionary philosophy has meant an acceptance of the view that change can occur in social organization and (by a natural step) an acceptance of the view that man can influence that change, governmental action being, of course, an important method of influencing the change.[18]

WHEN THE FUTURE COMES

And when we come to ask what may be expected from the future, what will be the shape of things to come, we find two commissions of social scientists, one appointed by a President of the United States to study social trends and another appointed by the American Historical Association, attempting to answer this question. The latter reported that:

Cumulative evidence supports the conclusion that, in the United States as in other countries, the age of individualism and *laissez-faire* in economy and government is closing and that a new age of collectivism is emerging.

As to the specific form which this "collectivism," this integration and interdependence, is taking and will take in the future, the evidence at hand is by no means clear or unequivocal. It may involve the limiting or supplanting of private property by public property or it may entail the preservation of private property, extended and distributed among the masses. Most likely, it will issue from a process of experimentation and will represent a composite of historic doctrines and social conceptions yet to appear. Almost certainly it will involve a larger measure of compulsory as well as voluntary co-operation of citizens in the conduct of the complex national economy, a corresponding enlargement of the functions of government, and an increasing state intervention in fundamental branches of economy previously left to individual discretion and initiative—a state intervention that in some instances may be direct and mandatory and in others indirect and facilitative. In any event the Commission is convinced by its inter-

[18] Marshall, *op. cit.*, Annals, 147, 7-8.

pretation of available empirical data that the actually integrating economy of the present day is the forerunner of a consciously integrated society in which individual economic actions and individual property rights will be altered and abridged.

The emerging age is particularly an age of transition. It is marked by numerous and severe tensions arising out of the conflict between the actual trend toward integrated economy and society, on the one side, and the traditional practices, dispositions, ideas, and institutional arrangements inherited from the passing age of individualism, on the other.[19]

President Hoover's commission on social trends reached the conclusion that:

Under such circumstances (as now exist in the United States) the problem of the interrelationship between government and industry is of grave importance. Shall business men become actual rulers; or shall rulers become industrialist; or shall labor and science rule the other rulers? Practically, the line between so-called "pure" economics and "pure" politics has been blurred in recent years by the events of the late war, and later by the stress of the economic depression. In each of these crises the ancient landmarks between business and government have been disregarded and new social boundaries have been accepted by acclamation. The actual question is that of developing quasi-governmental agencies and quasi-industrial agencies on the borders of the older economic and governmental enterprises, and of the freer intermingling of organization and personnel, along with the recognition of their interdependence in many relations.

Observers of social change may look here for the appearance of new types of politico-economic organization, new constellations of government, industry, and technology, forms now only dimly discerned; the quasi-governmental corporation, the government-owned corporation, the mixed corporation, the semi- and demi-autonomous industrial groupings in varying relations to the State. We may look for important developments alike in the concentration and in the devolution of social control, experiments perhaps in the direction of the self-government of various industries under central guidance, experiments in coöperation and accommodation between industry and government, especially as the larger units of industrial organization, coöperative and otherwise, become more like governments in personnel and budgets, and as governments become agencies of general welfare as well as of coercion.

The hybrid nature of some of these creations may be the despair of those theorists, both radical and conservative, who see the world only in terms of an unquestioning acceptance of one or the other of

[19] Report of the Commission on the Social Studies, *op. cit.*, pp. 16-17.

two exclusive dogmas, but these innovations will be welcomed by those who are less concerned about phobiasm than with the prompt and practical adjustment of actual affairs to the brutal realities of changing social and economic conditions. The American outcome, since all the possible molds of thought and invention have not yet been exhausted may be a type *sui generis* adapted to the special needs, opportunities, limitations, and genius of the American people.

Those who reason in terms of isms or of the theoretical rightness or wrongness of state activity may be profoundly perplexed by the range of governmental expansion or contraction, but the student of social trends observes nothing alarming in the widely varying forms of social adjustment undertaken by government, whether maternal, paternal, or fraternal, from one period to another.[20]

[20] From the report of the President's Research Committee, published in *Recent Social Trends in the United States*, I, lxii and lxiii. (2 vols., McGraw-Hill Book Company, 1933).